HANNAH'S PRAYER AND ITS ANSWER

Hannah's Prayer and Its Answer

AN EXPOSITION FOR BIBLE STUDY

Ronald S. Wallace

WILLIAM B. EERDMANS PUBLISHING COMPANY
GRAND RAPIDS, MICHIGAN / CAMBRIDGE, U.K.

RUTHERFORD HOUSE
EDINBURGH, U.K.

Published jointly 2002
in the United States of America by
Wm. B. Eerdmans Publishing Co.
255 Jefferson Ave. S.E., Grand Rapids, Michigan 49503
www.eerdmans.com
and in the U.K. by
Rutherford House
17 Claremont Park
Edinburgh EH6 7PJ

Printed in the United States of America

07 06 05 04 03 02   7 6 5 4 3 2 1

Library of Congress Cataloging-in-Publication Data

Hannah's prayer and its answer: an exposition for Bible study / Ronald S. Wallace.
p.   cm.
ISBN 0-8028-6068-0 (pbk.: alk. paper)
1. Bible. O.T. Samuel, 1st, I-VII — Criticism, interpretation, etc.
2. Prayer — Biblical teaching. I. Title.

BS1325.6.P68 2002
222′.4307 — dc21

2002023822

British Library Cataloguing-in-Publication Data

A catalogue record for this book
is available from the British Library

Rutherford House ISBN 0 946068 86 0

Unless otherwise noted, the Scripture quotations in this publication
are from the New Revised Standard Version of the Bible, copyright ©
1989 by the Division of Christian Education of the National Council of
Churches of Christ in the U.S.A., and used by permission.

In memory of
Annie E. Torrance
1883–1980
who prayed
and was answered

Contents

Contents

Contents

Contents

Acknowledgments

I have always regarded the first seven chapters of 1 Samuel, whatever the source of its composite sections, as designed to be the record of one distinctively important period in Israel's history. Some years ago I tried to bring this out in a series of expositions that were printed in the quarterly magazine *Evangel,* edited by Dr. Nigel Cameron. I have rewritten these for final publication in this book.

I am grateful to David C. Searle, warden of Rutherford House, for carefully editing the text and being so willing to sponsor a U.K. edition.

It is almost half a century ago that Wm. B. Eerdmans Publishing Co. began to republish in the U.S.A. one or two of my books then in print and to give them the best circulation I could desire. I am grateful that the valued friendship I then had with Mr. Bill Eerdmans Jr. has continued, and that recently he has taken wholly in hand the printing and publication of a couple of my books. I have been grateful for the care put into the production and the splendid appearance and quality of the finished volumes.

Preface

When the narrator, at the beginning of 1 Samuel, gave us so fully the details of Hannah's home and prayer life, one of his main purposes was eventually to bring home to us the importance and efficacy of prayer. It was in answer to the prayer and prophetic hope of this one humble and concerned woman that God blessed Israel in the birth of one of its most influential prophets. Samuel's achievement during the most active period of his life was to rescue Israel from the paganism of its blind leadership, its failed priesthood under Eli, its corrupt tabernacle worship, and its oppressive bondage under the Philistines. In his old age he was greatly used by God to orient the history of his people in a quite decisive way towards the hope of a future Messianic Son of David. Hannah with her piety and prayer is here given a place in Israel's history faintly similar to that of Mary in the New Testament. The seventh chapter is outstanding. It is obviously written to describe how, after much frustration and deep disappointment, Samuel's life-work was finally crowned with brilliant success in delivering, judging, and leading Israel.

When I began to expound 1 Samuel at my weekly prayer meeting during my early ministry it became my conviction that the first seven chapters, with their fascinating stories of various origins, had been skillfully arranged and woven together by the final editor in order to present us with one unified narrative, encouraging us not only in our personal prayer life but also in the even more important task of prayer for the church and society. Even though I hope eventually to cover the whole book, I have felt that this portion of it would make a satisfying and illuminating short series for individual or group Bible study.

CHAPTER I

The Making of a Prayer

1 Samuel 1:1-11

The Narrative

The family situation of Elkanah, a godly Israelite from an area with a pious tradition, was often spoiled and always tense with quarrels between his two wives. Hannah was childless, and Peninnah who had many offspring often taunted her about her condition, which was then commonly accepted as being due to God's disfavor. The tension became even more bitter during the annual visit to the Temple at Shiloh, for there Peninnah supported what Hannah abhorred — the shameful and degrading practices encouraged by the degenerate priests, the sons of Eli. We are told here of how, on one of these annual visits at the time of the sacrificial meal when Elkanah seemed to be giving special favor to Peninnah, Hannah broke away from the family circle to pray with inspired intensity for a male child whom she would dedicate from his earliest childhood to the true service of God in his Temple.

The Times

When Samuel was born, community life in Israel was becoming increasingly sordid and cruel. The establishment was hopelessly corrupt, political leadership incompetent, the morals of the people decadent. The rottenness had begun to show itself in the Temple services at Shiloh. Hophni and Phinehas, the sons and successors of Eli the high priest, were greedy, arrogant, and expert in priestcraft, and they did nothing to discourage the disorderly drinking habits and sexual license of the times even within the environs of the holy place. Their old father, still clinging to his high office though now blind, and powerless to reform anything, seemed alone to be ashamed at what was taking place around him. The book of Judges shows us why and how affairs had reached this state at this time. After the days of Joshua, Moses' successor, there had begun a century of general and gradual decline in morale and spiritual life. Each generation had adopted a scale of values lower than its predecessor, never imagining that things could have been different, or that reform was possible.

It is true that occasionally, here and there, we find that a few had not drifted with the crowd when the whole nation lost its bearings. These people, like a remnant of what had been once great, shone like bright lights in a very dark world. In the Book of Ruth, for example, we are told about

Naomi, Boaz, and their pious circle in the little town of Bethlehem. At the time now under review we meet a prophet, called a *"man of God,"* who appeared in the Temple with a message from the Lord. Among such people also we can number Elkanah of Ramathaim-Zophim of the hill country of Ephraim, and Hannah his wife. We can gather from the early chapters of the book of Samuel that Eli, the high priest who resided within the holy place at Shiloh, respected such people as Elkanah and Hannah. When they came around the Temple he did his best to encourage their zeal and to protect them from the corruption that was so widespread under his sons in the Temple courts.

Hannah Learns to Pray

Early in her married life Hannah went through a long period of excruciating suffering. She was childless, and her sorrow over her condition was made especially acute by the taunts of Peninnah, Elkanah's other wife, who produced enough sons and daughters amply to compensate for Hannah's barrenness, and who became more proud and insulting towards Hannah as she did so. The latter was greatly hurt also by the fact that even the good people of her day believed that barrenness in a woman was a sign that something in her life and attitude was displeasing to God. She felt both suspected and rejected.

Hannah found release for all her inner tension by seeking God's fellowship. Her affliction became a school of prayer for her. It drove her to prayer, taught her what prayer really is, and taught her how to pray. Shaped by her unique circumstances, her prayers were often intense and passionate. We will find, as we read on, that when she was challenged by Eli for being too emotional in her devotion, she explained very simply and sincerely what she was doing. *"I have been pouring out my soul before the LORD. . . . I have been speaking out of my great anxiety and vexation"* (1:15-16). She felt that even her husband, though he tried hard, was sometimes insensitive and did not understand (1:8). Yet she felt that the presence of God, as she opened up her heart and life to him, encouraged her to give vent to all her anxieties and complaints, holding nothing back in any dark recessed place of the soul or mind.

We are meant to appreciate the lesson. Prayer is described in the book of Psalms as the "pouring out of the heart" to God, and it is characteristic of genuine prayer in the Bible to be the spontaneous, free, and inspired utterance of the surrendered heart before the Lord, whatever the mood. Some psalms can be accurately described as prayers of complaint. Some are simply a string of lamentations uttered from a heart mourning before God. Some are lengthy confessions of sin when the psalmist felt overwhelmed with guilt. Some are utterances of pure delight and thanksgiving. Some are expressions of awe and fear. Several are freely uttered expressions of the psalmist's hatred of God's enemies, a hatred that he felt to be intensified the nearer he was to God (see, e.g., Ps. 139:19-22). Men and women found relief especially in the Temple by using such psalms to help them cast the burden of their feelings and moods on the Lord in this way. What they learned in the Temple they took back with them into ordinary life, where they found themselves able to turn to God in home and in field, to cast the overwhelming burden of their daily lives often on him.

The Enlargement of Her Vision and Concern

When we first meet her early in her married life in Ramathaim-Zophim we can understand how within the narrow and constricted world of her home, Hannah's prayers, like her sorrows and desires, may have been predominantly personal and private, perhaps in danger of becoming self-centered. She would continually lament her childlessness before the Lord; she would protest her innocence and yet at the same time ask him to show her where she might have displeased him. Often she must have pleaded with him to vindicate her by giving her the child she desired.

After some years, however, the world she lived in grew much larger, the problems facing her in life much more wide-ranging. In the battle she found herself engaged in, the issues were far more serious than she had ever before faced. All this will be brought out clearly as we move on in the story and read the great song of thanksgiving that marks the climax of her prayer life and spiritual pilgrimage. The song reveals her to us as a woman who has lived for many years burdened with a deep and anxious concern, not for herself but for God's cause and for the welfare of his people Israel.

The writer in this way is trying to show us how Hannah's mind was gradually taken over by these concerns that would later dominate her whole outlook and prayer life. He points out that it was especially during the annual family visit to the Temple that Hannah herself grew more unsatisfied and miserable, and the tension between her and her domestic rival grew more severe. We would have expected otherwise. Surely Hannah's yearly visit should have helped her settle with herself and brought her at least peace and contentment. Why was it that on each annual visit to the house of God she grew more restless, and the family quarrels more serious?

It is obvious that in those visits to the holy place at Shiloh, Hannah was gradually brought face to face with problems far more urgent than those of her own home circle, and she was introduced to a sorrow more acute than her own sense of rejection. There she saw with her own eyes the degrading Temple practices, the blatant self-seeking of the younger priests, the arrogance of their servants. There she began to think how God must feel — the God of Abraham, Jacob, and Moses! She thought about the love he had lavished upon those very people, and the glory he had meant them to inherit. As she took it all into her mind and heart she began to feel a shame and concern that came to her not only from sharing God's outlook, but also from fellowship with his heart. She felt moreover that she had been given this fellowship with God, and this burden of his shame and concern, because he was calling her into his service in this crisis, especially to the service of praying.

Her sorrow about her childlessness thus became wholly reoriented. It no longer revolved around the pleasure a child

any truth ?
here

might give to her husband or to herself, but around her desire for God's glory. She saw that the situation in Israel required, above all, a leader, a prophet of God like Moses who could be a new deliverer — one who could rebuke the evils of his day, preach the truth, and call the whole nation to repentance. Her desire now was to bear a child not simply to give pleasure to her husband, or to save her own reputation or to defeat her rival, but to be the man of God who could put things right in her time. If the custom of the day had allowed her, she would herself have become that prophet and leader. In the prayer for a son she was saying her utmost to God and saying it with complete self-effacement, "Lord, here I am. Send me."

Hannah's great song of thanksgiving shows us also that, as she looked around her in the Temple, she was not only burdened with a great concern for God's cause, but she was also challenged to what she believed was a justifiable and burning anger over the situation before her. Certainly there were many around her who were like lost sheep to be pitied for the darkness, ignorance, and misery of their condition and ways. But in the high places of the nation she saw that many were making profit from the godlessness of the times, perverting justice, deliberately destroying decency and order, finding satisfaction in their evil achievements, and triumphing as the avowed enemies of the Lord. Such people and powers had to be destroyed if the true Israel of God was to be retrieved. Hannah began to hate what was taking place around her and to hate those who were responsible for it. She felt, indeed, that behind her own sense of indignation there was something of God's own hatred of evil and injustice. In the house of the Lord she wanted the oppressive power of the mighty to be broken, the poor and needy raised from the dust (2:4, 7-8). This is why the writer points out that these annual visits to the Temple increased not only Hannah's grief but also the family tension. We have already suggested that Peninnah, like many other respectable people of the day, approved of the "progressive permissiveness" of their generation and, as she discovered Hannah's mind, was thus provoked to become all the more scornful of Hannah's naïve and futile conservatism.

Hannah thus in her praying began to bring to God the sorrows and shame of the world around her. She spoke no more merely out of personal *"anxiety and vexation"* but out of great religious and social concern and indignation. Prayer thus gradually became the pouring out of her heart's desire in intercession that everything around her should be brought back under the rule and law of God. In her praying she expressed her antagonism at what was hindering the fulfillment of God's will in the world around her. Her mind, heart, and will had fiercely rebelled against the blasphemous wrongs and obscenities. She found in prayer before God a field in which she could enter into conflict with God's enemies and pray for their defeat and destruction, engaging in what has been called a "mental strife." She felt that this was a way in which what is alien to God's will could be overcome. She believed that he would not only hear but also answer those who thus sought his glory and his kingdom. Hannah's first concern in praying therefore became: "Hallowed be thy name, thy kingdom come. Thy will be done on earth as it is in heaven."

One Day, in One Petition!

We are told that for a long time — indeed, *"year by year"* — Hannah almost fell into a routine of praying on and on, without anything happening around her to show that her prayers were being effective. No doubt she felt the presence of God and had some assurance in her mind that she was being heard. No doubt too, her praying became more intense and urgent as year followed year. Yet no sign or word was ever given to her about any possible immediate outcome of her praying: *"So it went on year by year[,] as often as she went up to the house of the LORD."*

Suddenly, however, the *"year by year"* routine was broken and things changed. We are told in detail how it happened. She broke down during a family meal. She *"wept and would not eat"* (v. 7). Elkanah tried to help but in spite of his pleading and assurance she fled. She hurried to the place in the Temple (see Additional Note at end of chapter) where she had often found quietness and comfort. It was in the inner sanctuary which Eli guarded and kept clear from the alien influences he knew his sons and their adherents were encouraging. Hannah had always liked the old man and had felt his presence to be a help. That day *"before the LORD"* with a boldness that was new to her, the impulse came to focus her desire on one particular request which she put more clearly and decisively than she had ever before attempted in her praying. We are given the gist of what she said in two formal sentences: *"O LORD of hosts, if thou wilt indeed look on the affliction of thy maidservant, and remember me, and not forget thy maidservant, but wilt give to thy maidservant a son, then I will give him to the Lord all the days of his life, and no razor shall touch his head"* (v. 11, RSV).

She is now no longer content to wait indefinitely, leaving it always to God to decide exactly what must happen. She is pressing God here and now to make the decisive action that she herself feels that the situation demands. She is determined moreover to show him the kind of way she would have things done. She tells him exactly what she feels and wants. She makes her plan, vows a vow about the part she will play in it, and proposes to God that it should happen soon. Then she challenges him to test her and see if she will not fulfill her part. Her prayer was uttered inwardly with intense emotion and fervency of will. She *"was praying silently; only her lips moved, but her voice was not heard"* (v. 13). As she *"continued praying before the Lord"* (v. 12), was she not at this point holding on to him as Jacob once did and refusing to let him go till she had some answer? She wants a definite reply to a definite request, and with all the eagerness and zeal she can muster she is making it as difficult as possible for him to disappoint her.

The teaching of Jesus himself seems to give us a clear approach to prayer in which the example of Hannah becomes a relevant and helpful illustration. Though Jesus' own prayer life was certainly based on his close communion with God, this was a communion that found frequent expression in asking God to do things. He thus encouraged us to make requests with like faith: "Ask, and it will be given you" (Luke 11:9; John 15:7; 16:23-24).

He insisted that we must not doubt in our heart as we ask (Mark 11:23; cf. Matt. 9:28). Indeed, if we believe that we are to receive what we ask, this very confidence will inspire God to answer (Mark 11:24). He underlined God's sympathy with our personal needs and his readiness to help us. He tried to create within us the same expectancy as would be awakened in a trustful child by the love of an earthly father.

Moreover our prayers should not become merely the routine expression of general wishful thinking. He encouraged us to fix on particulars, to mention specific matters even in their concrete details, and to suggest ways in which we feel God should go about doing what we request. "If two of you agree on earth about anything you ask, it will be done for you by my Father in heaven" (Matt. 18:19). By his use of words such as "anything" and "whatsoever" (Matt. 18:19; John 16:23, AV; cf. Mark 11:24) in his instructions about what we can bring before him in prayer, he seems intentionally to have left open to us a wide field of choice. His encouragement to us to form such definite requests is often reinforced by promises that our prayers will be answered: what we ask "will be given" or "will be done" (Matt. 7:7; 18:19; Mark 11:23).

Of course he made it clear that these great words of encouragement to ask and to be definite and pressing as we do so, are addressed only to those who in their lives are committed wholly to his service and who will never seek to apply his teaching in order to fill their lives with sheer self-centered trivialities. We must ask in his name, and according to his Word (John 16:23-24). "If you abide in me," he said, "and my words abide in you, ask for whatever you wish" (John 15:7).

In this matter too, Hannah remains a healthy model. Of course the human freedom and initiative that she dared to

take in uttering her petition are inspired by God himself. Yet
in God's presence she does not dare to become presumptu-
ous. She is his "servant," completely surrendered to him. We
can imagine her even trembling as she speaks to him, yet it
is the same divine presence that also makes her bold. She
feels she is on good ground indeed as she lays open her
heart and discusses with him so intimately, exactly what she
wants as a solution of the problem that belongs to both her
and him. She presses him to understand and give his answer. Here as we listen to Hannah praying we can understand how in Old Testament times, though they knew God
to be "the Holy One, high and lifted up who inhabits eter-
nity," they knew too that he who dwells in the high and holy
place dwells also with them who are of a humble and con-
trite heart, that he inspires and hears their personal requests, and sometimes prepares exactly the kind of place for
them in his service that he has led their hearts to desire.

"Pray Without Ceasing"

Of all the lessons taught here about prayer we must return
before we conclude this chapter to the one most relevant to
our present-day situation. As we follow the story of Israel in
the Bible from the beginning of the book of Samuel to the
coming of Christ, we discover that what took place in answer to that one particular prayer proved to be a turning
point, not only in the life of Hannah herself but also in the
life of the people of God. Her child Samuel became the
prophet whose ministry was to open up an entirely new era

of hope and fulfillment in Israel's living and, indeed, in world affairs. We ourselves are challenged, as often throughout the Bible, to grasp the importance of the kind of intercession that Hannah here began to take as her life work.

God loves to have the human situation entered, taken up, and brought before him in all its urgency and seriousness by people who are willing to share his own sense of righteousness, to burden their hearts with the needs of the community around them, and to pressure him, as Hannah did, with their concern and desires. It was for this purpose that he raised up prophets in Israel. They were there not only to preach but to pray. They were to "stand before the Lord" in intercession for the people. They were to be like watchmen set on the walls of Jerusalem so that "all day and all night they shall never be silent," giving the Lord "no rest until he establishes Jerusalem" (Isa. 62:6, 7). God grieved when they failed in their task — when he looked, saw wrongdoing, ignorance, and folly prevalent among his people, and yet heard from the midst of them no intercessory cry of protest or prayer — as if no one cared (Isa. 59:16)!

Of course God also enters the human situation himself directly. He *knows* everything about our human need. There is no act of indecency or injustice on this earth that is not marked by him, no one in whatever depth of misery whose tears are not numbered and whose pain is not felt. He saw the affliction and heard the cry of his persecuted people in Egypt long before he sent Moses among them to be his ambassador and intercessor (Exod. 3:7). He heard the pathetic crying of the boy Ishmael in the desert when even his mother in despair had given him up as doomed to death

(Gen. 21:16-17). Yet God loves it especially if one prays for another because one cares for another. He has a special place in his heart and purposes for those who, like Hannah, will give themselves to prayer for the welfare of the people of God.

In his ministry of intercession the prophet Jeremiah came very close to Hannah as we have described her. What drove him to pray for his countrymen following his call to preach the Word of God was his emotional sensitivity to the state of affairs he found among the people of his day as he moved among them. He discovered, as no other prophet before him had ever done, the immense and innate power of human wickedness. He expressed the conviction that there was no sorrow on earth like the burden of caring people who are near to God, and have begun to understand God's feelings, as they look around them on the devastation and ugliness that sin has worked in the life of the people of God (cf. Lam. 1:12).

> O that my head were a spring of water,
> and my eyes a fountain of tears,
> so that I might weep day and night
> for the slain of my poor people! (Jer. 9:1)

It is a remarkable fact of Bible history that Hannah — so many years before Jeremiah — showed the same clear prophetic vision of the human situation and gave herself the same kind of ministry of caring and intercession for the kingdom of God in an age that had forgotten him. The prophets stand out in the Bible as rather distant, exceptional figures especially called for an outstanding task.

Hannah is close to us. She was an ordinary person fulfilling the humble vocation of housewife. She was no expert in spirituality, in the probing of mystical experiences. All she did and achieved was done without any dramatic call to do it, and under circumstances remarkably similar to those that prevail everywhere in the Western world today.

Additional Note on the Sanctuary at Shiloh

The tent of meeting used during the wilderness wanderings had been given by Joshua a permanent location at Shiloh (Josh. 18:1). The author of Psalm 78 appears to suggest that when the Ark was stolen by the Philistines, the tent of meeting was at that point destroyed: "He abandoned the tabernacle of Shiloh, the tent he had set up among men; he sent the ark of his might into captivity, his splendor into the hands of the enemy" (vv. 60-61, NIV). However, the phrase used in verse 9, *"the doorpost of the temple of the LORD,"* suggests a more permanent building and other doors are referred to in 3:15. Since no trace of any Temple building has been found in excavations at the site of Shiloh, it is possible that the tent of meeting had been replaced or supplemented by a wooden structure to house the Ark and maintain Shiloh's place as Israel's main sanctuary (cf. 3:3). However, in the light of God's word to Nathan in 2 Samuel 7:6, it would appear that something of the tent of meeting still survived.

CHAPTER 2

The Answer, the Sacrifice, and the Song

1 Samuel 1:12–2:11

The Narrative

Eli at first completely misinterpreted Hannah's intensity in prayer, rebuking her for her apparent self-abandonment to emotion, even accusing her of being a drunken prostitute. We are told of her self-defense, and of Eli's repentance, then of how he uttered the prophetic word that assured her beyond all doubt that God would honor her faith and give her the answer. Then came the journey home, the promised birth, and Hannah's decision, with Eli's understanding and consent, to postpone the next visit to the Temple until the child was ready to be weaned and taken there finally to grow up under Eli as a priest in the service of the Lord.

In delivering the child, as vowed, both parents made a costly sacrifice. Hannah, overcome again with emotion, recognizing how marvelously God was furthering the promised salvation of Israel, burst into a great and memorable song of praise, self-vindication, and triumph.

The Word of Peace and Power

Many of the prayers in the book of Psalms and elsewhere in the Bible end on a note of assurance, sometimes quiet, sometimes exultant. God has been there with a word, and has inspired a triumphant faith that things will be well. Indeed we can sometimes trace a point in the prayer itself where the climate of the mind was wondrously changed. As Hannah *"continued praying before the LORD"* (v. 12) she hoped that her prayer, too, would take such a turn and have such an end. She wanted, too, the liberty to go back to her husband and home knowing that she could cope more fully with what had vexed her too much. So intense was her waiting on God for all this that she refused to let herself become upset or even diverted when Eli, thinking she was a drunken woman, and probably shaking her, bent down and shouted in her ear, *"Enough of this drunken behaviour,"* and told her to *"go away till the wine has worn off"* (v. 14, NEB).

We can understand the concern Eli felt when he saw Hannah's movements. He was trying to maintain a discipline that would exclude from this part of the Temple the pagan immorality that was being fostered elsewhere even by his sons. No doubt he believed, too, that he was justified in being suspicious of what he regarded as an overemotional type of piety. Yet his clumsy pastoral blunder is a warning to us even today. When God's Spirit is at work in a human personality, the word spoken by Jesus to Nicodemus is always relevant: "The wind blows where it chooses, and you hear the sound of it, but you do not know where it comes from or where it goes" (John 3:8). No matter how well-trained and experienced we may be, our attempts to discover what is really going on beneath the surface when a human soul is being awakened and reoriented by the Spirit of God will often leave us completely baffled.

Eli was indeed saved from pursuing a foolish mistake to what would have been seriously damaging consequences, by the sweetness and patience of Hannah herself when she finally replied to him. And if we blame him for his stupid brashness, we must at least credit the speed with which he learned his lesson (and that from a member of his congregation), and the way he made amends. Quietly praying to God for forgiveness, he there and then pronounced on Hannah a priestly blessing. The formal words may have seemed superficial to an onlooker: *"Go in peace; the God of Israel grant the petition you have made to him"* (v. 17). For Hannah, however, it was one of the greatest moments of her life. In the voice of Eli, she heard the voice of God. He was saying, "I have heard you and I understand. You are mine! Trust me with your prayers, your hopes, your words, your plans, your home, your future, and your nation."

The word brought a final peace. It suddenly healed what had hurt her *"year by year"* (v. 7). From that moment she knew that all was well with the cause for which she had prayed and suffered so much. Of course she had no proof, not even a sign — only a word. Yet certainty was there in the word that had been spoken. *"The woman went her way and ate, and her countenance was no longer sad"* (v. 18, RSV). She went *"her way"* — back to Ramah, back to Elkanah and the routine of each day within her little world, yet she now had the power to overcome her every little domestic vexation. Moreover, she knew beyond doubt that Israel would be restored and the Lord's enemies judged.

At this point the story can be about ourselves if we will have it. We can compare it with what happened when the nobleman from Capernaum in desperate need sought out Jesus at Cana and asked him to go home with him to cure his son. Jesus there and then gave him no sign. He did not try even to go along the road with him. He gave him simply a word: "Go; your son will live." Yet the mere hearing of the word brought the man as much assurance as if he had already seen the miracle. "The man believed the word that Jesus spoke to him and started on his way" (John 4:46-53). If we believe and know that Jesus Christ is the same yesterday, today, and forever, and that his sheep still hear his voice, we can surely expect to hear such a word for ourselves in face of whatever overwhelming problem this life brings to us. How much we would find in our churchgoing if we could only hear there from week to week such a word for our need — and this is what God means to happen! Eli may have had his serious failings, and he was a man of ordinary ability, but by God's grace he was able at least once to speak such a word, when he began repentantly to pray for help to do so.

The Miracle

"The LORD remembered [Hannah]" (v. 19). He remembered her because she had been there before him in the time of prayer. He remembered how she dedicated herself to his service, vowed her vow, made her petition. He remembered the devotion of a heart burdened with the same love as he himself felt for his people Israel. God never forgets those warm close moments that take place between himself and those he calls into his fellowship and service. Indeed he dwells on them in his memory.

> I remember the devotion of your youth,
>   your love as a bride,
> how you followed me in the wilderness. . . .
>
> (Jer. 2:2)

How tragic it is that the fellowship which means so much to God, we can deem so cheap! We allow the passing of time too easily to take its toll, to play havoc with our memory of God's friendship to us and to divert our loyalty. Our hearts grow cold and weary too. "I have this against you: you have lost your early love" (Rev. 2:4, NEB), was the Lord's complaint against the church at Ephesus. Having allowed the vision to fade, and the warmth to cool off, we all the more firmly assert our preference for a religion that is doctrinal and practical rather than emotional.

"In due time Hannah conceived and bore a son. She named him Samuel, for she said, 'I have asked him of the LORD'" (v. 20). It can be argued that there was nothing miraculous about the

birth of Samuel. In the events that followed Hannah's prayer, everything that occurred followed a normal course. No laws of nature were broken: *"Elkanah knew his wife Hannah,"* and the child was born *"in due time"* (vv. 19-20). Some doctors would say today that what made the difference on Hannah's part was that now she had learned to relax! For Hannah, however, everything about the birth was sheer miracle. She remembered the word, and the prayer: *"I have asked him of the LORD"* (v. 20). If Samuel had been given to her without the human agency of her husband the event would have been no more marvelous in her eyes. The thing that had happened in her life, she believed, was due to the word that God had spoken.

Within the apparent chaos of events that take place around us, can there not also occur certain events that happen wonderfully and unpredictably because we ourselves, or others, pray to God? God hears and gives his word so that his kingdom advances and his purposes are furthered. Such events, viewed superficially, may be very ordinary. Sometimes they can be extraordinary. A miracle is an event, whether brought about by ordinary or extraordinary means, that happens with the most precise timing through such a specially given and determined word of God, in order to further his redeeming purposes and to bring in his kingdom.

Prayer, for Hannah, was a life-work. The renewal of Israel which was the real and final answer to her praying was delayed by at least a generation before it was brought about. Perhaps Hannah did not live to see it. Yet this miracle encouraged her and helped her to believe and to continue praying. It was a sign that she was being heard. It was followed later by other signs of God's blessing and favor as Samuel grew and began his ministry, and as other children were born to her. God kept her going and kept her praying.

Praying is meant to be a life-work today. All prayers are meant to be given in the content of one great prayer which we must never cease to pray — "Thy kingdom come!" Of course as we pray it, we are encouraged to pray that God might bring about change here and there around us — in certain persons' thoughts and attitudes, in health, and in life-direction. These are the signs and accompaniments of the coming of his kingdom. It can help us to continue to pray, "Thy kingdom come," if in some of the mundane areas of life around us we can notice how powerfully and intimately God is at work already. Are we not daily being laden with good things, and are we ever left desolate? Can we not sometimes discern, in what others would call mere coincidences, the workings of his love and power which we ourselves can never attribute to mere chance? Archbishop Temple is quoted as saying, "When prayers cease, coincidences cease."

The Sacrifice

Hannah remembered not only God's word, but her own vow: *"I will give him to the LORD for all the days of his life, and no razor will ever by used on his head"* (v. 11, NIV). There could be now no questioning, no thought of taking back what she herself had said. The story of Jephthah was well known to her. She would do as she meant when she spoke. She would nurse him, and when he was weaned, after three years, he would go to the Temple to be put under the care of Eli.

Of course by our present-day standards we would raise serious questions about the right or the wisdom of a parent to dedicate a child so early to serve in a religious order, or to leave a three-year-old at a preparatory school where he could easily encounter moral danger. We can imagine, too, a bitter resentment developing within the heart of the growing child — abandoned by his mother and deprived of her love so early. Many commentators feel that because of such early treatment, Samuel's character became harsh. We must not, however, blind ourselves to the need and the duty of parents at least to make vows and promises before God on behalf of the children. In the Old Testament world Israel's survival depended on the parents passing on to their children the faith of their forebears, and on children accepting what was given and taught.

What Hannah did in fulfilling her extraordinary vow, however, requires special justification, and we can only look on her case as an extreme exception to a rule. In the Bible we read of God's commanding and allowing things that we ourselves could not dare to think of doing on our own initiative. We must therefore accept the possibility that God himself had a part in the inspiration of Hannah's vow; and through this involvement also pledged himself to look after Samuel's upbringing, and to give exceptional grace to overcome the dangers that to our modern minds were so great. The fact that Hannah did prepare herself immediately to fulfill this fearful vow shows how strong her conviction was when it was made, that her prayer was indeed divinely inspired. It proves, too, how certain she now was that its answer was entirely from God. Was it not possible that Hannah, when she made her vow, was thinking of the sacrifice of Isaac on Mount Moriah? Abraham in his old age had already been through test after test as to whether he would give up everything he had to God, but now God said, "One more test, Abraham. Give me Isaac"! God was pleased when Abraham obeyed and did not withhold his dearest son, his greatest hope and the supreme fruit of his long life of sacrifice. Was not Hannah, in making her inspired vow, saying, "Lord, if you will give me a son for your service, as you gave Isaac to father Abraham, then I too will lay him on the altar before you as Abraham laid his son Isaac on the altar on the mountain?"

That Hannah was thinking of Abraham in the way we have indicated can explain why during the first three years after his birth she refused to go up from her village to the Temple at Shiloh. She knew that the sacrifice of the child when she made it would cost her no less an agony than that which came to Abraham, not only on the mountain when he bound Isaac to the altar and raised his knife, but also on the long three-day journey. Could God expect more from her than he took from Abraham? She would go up only once and she asked God to spare her and let her stay at home till the day came when she *had* to pay her vow.

It is illuminating to see how Elkanah now tries to help Hannah when she told him that she had decided to postpone her visits to the Temple. No doubt he has come to appreciate that she has lived nearer to God than he himself has done. Of course the child is his too, yet he subjects himself to her wishes. The story indeed shows that Hannah is as free before her husband as she has been free before God. When he discusses her problem with her he proves that he understands the sufferings she will go through. He tries to be one with her in the sacrifice she is going to make, and he prays with her that since God himself inspired her vow he will give her strength to fulfill it. *"Do what you think fit; wait until you have weaned him. May Yahweh bring about what you have said"* (v. 23, Jerusalem Bible).

Elkanah's prayer was marvelously answered on the great day when finally they took him up with his little bundle of clothes and chattels to leave him, as they firmly believed, in the hands of the Lord. To symbolize what they were doing they took a sacrifice that in relation to their worldly possessions would be reckoned costly. No doubt the three-year-old bull was to be slain at the altar as a ransom to redeem the firstborn of Hannah's womb, but in making the offering of the animal to God they must have felt they were laying themselves and their child wholly on God's altar for whatever purpose he now willed for them. When *"they brought the child to Eli"* (v. 25), Hannah recalled to him the great moment of her life when he helped her to find her freedom as a child of God. *"Oh, my lord!"* she said to the old priest. *"As you live, my lord, I am the woman who was standing here in your presence, praying to the LORD"* (v. 26). She told him her story and confessed her faith: *"For this child I prayed, and the LORD has granted me the petition that I made to him"* (v. 27). She reaffirmed her vow and her belief that the boy could not but live up to the name she had given to him. *"Therefore I have lent him to the LORD; as long as he lives, he is given to the LORD"* (v. 28). In these words we can begin to sense the thrill of great joy that came to her at that very moment. As they worshiped together at the altar she burst out in her exultant song of triumph.

The Song

Hannah's song begins with an exultant confession of faith. It takes us to the heart of her own personal relationship with God and shows us where the devotion of her soul rested, and where she drew her strength.

> My heart exults in the LORD;
> my strength is exalted in my God." (2:1a)

She in no way depended on her feelings. She knew that her present mood might be short-lived. Tomorrow she would be going back home without her little boy. She would have to live in close encounter with a Peninnah now accusing her of cruelty towards the child. She might be tempted to depression. Therefore even in her moment of joy she looks entirely away from herself. Her faith is *"in the LORD."* Her joy comes entirely from the goodness she has seen there in *him.* Her assurance rests on his promises. She lives by what she knows him to be.

> My mouth derides my enemies,
> because I rejoice in thy salvation. (v. 1b, RSV)

When she mentions "salvation" here she is certainly speaking out of her own heartfelt experience, but she is also

27

continuing to look away from herself and her circumstances. She is thinking, rather, of God's own saving deeds in history. The sight of her little one being installed as a priest in the service of God under the care of Eli lifted her mind entirely beyond any doubt that very soon the course of her nation's history would be changed. She remembered the promises given first to Abraham, and repeated often by Moses about the glorious future of the children of Israel, and as she looked there at Samuel she seemed to see them all fulfilled. This little boy whom she was giving to the Lord would be the leader who would put all his enemies to flight. He would soon cleanse the Temple and its priesthood. He would be the prophet who would bring the whole nation back to the faith it had deserted. She had no sign that such a transformation was about to take place except this first token answer that God had given to her prayer. The enemies of the Lord around her seemed to be as healthy and powerful as they had ever been — and yet she saw them all broken and helpless, and she proclaimed their certain and imminent doom. Their gods, too, would perish with them. She exalts the Lord over against the futile and empty male and female Baal gods of Canaan to which so many around her were being drawn:

> There is no Holy One like the LORD,
>   no one besides you;
>   there is no Rock like our God.   (v. 2)

There are hints in the song, especially towards the end, that even while her mind was chiefly occupied with such coming historical events, like the great prophets she too was given a glimpse of a more distant and ultimate event in which God would bring salvation not simply for Israel but for all the ends of the earth, and would end the reign of falsehood and pride for all nations. In her case it was only a fleeting vision of what other prophets were able at times to describe with much greater fullness. Yet it is a remarkable fact that her song was a prophecy standing on the border between the Old Testament and the New.

No one familiar with the Bible can fail to move in imagination from Hannah in the Old Testament to Simeon in the New. Like Hannah, Simeon was "righteous and devout, looking forward to the consolation of Israel" (Luke 2:25). The Holy Spirit had revealed to him that before he died he would see the Lord's Messiah. He was divinely prompted to go into the Temple when Jesus' parents brought him, as Hannah and Elkanah brought Samuel, their firstborn, to be presented to the Lord with the prescribed offerings. When Simeon took the child Jesus in his arms the Spirit came upon him, and he too seemed to see a glorious future for Israel and the world unfolded before his eyes. He broke into an exultant song:

> "Master, now you are dismissing your servant in peace,
>   according to your word;
> for my eyes have seen your salvation,
>   which you have prepared in the presence
>   of all peoples,
> a light for revelation to the Gentiles
>   and for glory to your people Israel."   (Luke 2:29-32)

In blessing he said, "This child is destined for the falling and rising of many in Israel" (v. 34).

Hannah is not directly mentioned by name in the New Testament. Indeed she is given no place in the catalog of Old Testament saints in the eleventh chapter of Hebrews. Yet the virgin Mary when she was blessed by Elizabeth broke out into song — the Magnificat — which contains so many echoes of the song of Hannah that it can be called simply a New Testament edition of it. She must have been very familiar with the whole story of Hannah. Elizabeth and Zechariah, too, must have felt that their son John was destined to fulfill much the same kind of mission in Israel as Samuel did in his time.

It is worth noting that when Hannah tried to give expression to her exuberant feelings as she worshiped before the Lord, she used the language of the traditional religious poetry of her day. It is possible indeed that she here may have simply repeated an older song celebrating some past victory in Israel's history. She had been taught it, perhaps as a child, and felt that it now applied exactly to her present situation. It is also possible that she composed the psalm herself using phrases and texts familiar to her through the liturgy of her day. Originally such expressions were coined to express the extraordinary feelings of triumph and ecstasy that occasionally marked the life and experience of the Old Testament prophets, psalmists, and people of God. Hannah may have felt that the use of such language alone could enable her to give adequate expression to her exhilaration, to the laughter of her soul, to the relief and liberation she was experiencing.

A Turning Point in History

The point at which the story of Hannah is placed in the biblical narrative is of great significance. Before she took her stand and made her vows and prayers in the Temple, the history of Israel (as we read it in the book of Judges) had been one of moral and spiritual decline, a decline going on from generation to generation, and lasting more than a century. What faced Hannah in her day was a situation on which experts in historical study would give the verdict "hopeless."

What took place, however, through her ministry of prayer under these very circumstances was the beginning of a great renewal in Israel's fortunes, the story of which occupies most of the two books of Samuel. Within one generation Israel recovered its faith, vision, and destiny. By the end of a second generation, Zion the city of God has been founded and built and David's throne has been established. The Word of God is being heard, the new Temple is planned, and people are being taught again to look forward to a greater glory yet to come. God is extolled for the triumph he has given to his king and the steadfast love he will show to David and his descendants forever (2 Sam. 22:51).

Hannah therefore occupies a place of great importance in the Bible. Certainly there are many other narratives in which we read of occasional prayer being raised to God and being answered dramatically. We read of battles being won, people being healed, the dead being raised, food and water being suddenly provided when prayer for such things was made. It is good to know that if we trust in God and pray, he has promised even through the giving of such stories to hear and answer. In the story of Hannah, however, we are reminded that God has given us prayer for a purpose much greater than that of occasionally helping us out when we are in dire trouble. God has given us the way of prayer as a service to God himself and the glory of his name. He wills that his purposes with his people and the fulfillment of his promise to bless all nations should be furthered by the efforts his people make in prayer. Jesus himself when he told us in our praying to say, "Thy kingdom come," was reminding us of this very fact: that God wants us to pray that the history of this world might always move in the right direction and that God seems to depend on our making such prayers.

In the second psalm, which scholars tell us may have been used at the coronation ceremony of the kings in Israel, one of the important commands given to the newly installed monarch was, "Ask of me, and I will make the nations your heritage, and the ends of the earth your possession" (Ps. 2:8). In the book of Ezekiel, in the thirty-sixth chapter, we have a vivid picture given to us of a people of God cleansed from sin, given a new heart and a new Spirit to walk in the ways of God, rebuilding, reinhabiting what has been desolate and making a garden of Eden out of waste places so that all nations come to know that their God is the Lord. Such a description is followed at the end of the chapter by the challenge and promise: "I will also let the house of Israel ask me to do this for them" (Ezek. 36:37). Here in the story of Hannah we are helped to understand what it means to make such a challenge in prayer seriously, and to act up to it in a determined and disciplined manner. She was no activist. She arranged no demonstrations. She preached no sermons. She served God simply through her suffering, prayer, and through an obscure act of personal yet costly and total self-sacrifice. She won an important battle for Israel's future, alone on her knees and in her heart before God. The writer means us to see that the renewal he is going to describe is brought about by such hidden passion and intercession as much as it is by the apparently more direct and effective activity in the field of public affairs.

Prophetic Warning and Comfort

While she proclaimed her vision of the coming salvation, like a true prophet, Hannah spoke of the doom that would inevitably come to those who resisted its advent.

The evils of her day were so deeply rooted in the social fabric that the rule of God could never be re-established in the life of the nation by any smooth and gradual process of re-education and persuasion. The coming of God's rule would mean radical and perhaps violent upheaval for those people and powers who in their defiant and arrogant atheism stood in the way of change. She therefore warns Hophni and Phinehas and their supporters that they will have no refuge when God comes to deal with them. Their hidden sins are already discovered by a God of judgment!

> Talk no more so very proudly,
>   let not arrogance come from your mouth;
> for the LORD is a God of knowledge,
>   and by him actions are weighed.   (v. 3)

She vividly describes what is to happen: *"Strong men stand in mute dismay"* while those who at present have plenty will *"sell themselves for a crust"* (v. 4, NEB). Those who at present think that the future belongs to them and their children will find themselves utterly forlorn (v. 5). Hannah is here speaking exactly as the later prophets of Israel spoke. She is speaking like Amos when he warned the oppressors and the proud in Israel to prepare to meet their God (cf. Amos 4:12). Her whole message is summed up in verses 6 and 7:

> The LORD kills and brings to life;
>> he brings down to Sheol and raises up.
> The LORD makes poor and makes rich;
>> he brings low, he also exalts.

Here she seems to be summing up the philosophy of history which, after long and sometimes bitter experiences of preaching God's word, came to characterize the thought of many of the great prophets of Israel. Often, at the beginning of the ministry they had glorious visions of the future that was in store for God's people. But as their ministry progressed and they began to experience rejection and hostility, they discovered that it was futile to expect renewal or reformation till the nation had first undergone a shattering experience of judgment. Isaiah even during his call was told that his preaching would not have any positive effect "until cities lie waste without inhabitant, and houses without people, and the land is utterly desolate" (Isa. 6:11). Ezekiel's words of warning to the last of the kings of Judah are reminiscent of those Hannah uttered in face of the corrupt ruling priesthood at Shiloh: "Remove the turban, take off the crown; things shall not remain as they are. Exalt that which is low, abase that which is high. A ruin, a ruin, a ruin — I will make it! (Such has never occurred.) Until he comes whose right it is; to him I will give it" (Ezek. 21:26-27).

The great prophets, when they proclaimed judgment to come, often spoke words of assurance and comfort to those whom they sometimes called a "remnant" who would remain faithful to God in the midst of the coming tribulation. So Hannah has a word for God's *"faithful ones."* Even those who trust and serve God will find themselves brought low. They will not escape the tribulations that will come upon the whole community. They will be made poor and will hunger when poverty and famine visit others. They will know what it means to tremble and even to suffer in the midst of a community under the devastating power of God's judgments. Yet they will have light in the midst of darkness and life in the midst of death. Hannah makes this promise of help definite and circumstantial: *"He will guard the feet of his faithful ones"* (v. 9). The picture is like that given in the 119th psalm, of a people going forward in surrounding darkness yet with a light at their feet enabling them to take one step at a time safely without fear of falling (Ps. 119:105). Though God is terrible in the judgments he can inflict, he is not ruthless or indiscriminate. He will care for the little flock who look to him and listen for his word. *"The feeble gird on strength"* (v. 4). *"Those who were hungry will hunger no more"* (v. 5, NIV). *"He raises up the poor from the dust"* (v. 8). How close we are in this song to the Beatitudes: "Blessed are those who mourn, for they will be comforted. Blessed are the meek, for they will inherit the earth. Blessed are those who hunger and thirst for righteousness, for they will be full" (Matt. 5:4ff.).

Hannah knew, even when she sang her song, that God had already planted and was nourishing and protecting within the life of Israel the seeds of a new kingdom that would grow, stand, and last forever. She herself in her own mind, heart, and womb had already experienced the presence and power of this new realm in that God had inspired, heard, and answered her prayers. She believed that her little boy Samuel would be shielded by God's grace as he grew to fulfill the ministry to which he was called. He would lead the true people of God into a new attitude and a new way of thinking and living through the coming crisis.

CHAPTER 3

Eli and His Sons

1 Samuel 2:12–3:1a

The Narrative

It is only now that Samuel has been installed as a growing influence for change that our imagination is allowed fully to hear about the despicable nature of the corruption that has entered so many aspects of the service of God in the Temple at Shiloh under the influence of Hophni and Phinehas, the sons of Eli. As the narrative unfolds the depth and power of the prevailing evils, the narrator, however, several times makes mention of how, in the midst of it all, Samuel is growing up in favor both with God and man, ultimately to take over. The climax of the narrative comes in a prophecy uttered by a man of God to Eli, who has failed to rebuke his sons effectively. It brought him the news that the hereditary priesthood that had given him and his predecessors such high status and responsibility in Israel was now to be discontinued; his sons were to be slain and his further descendants would reap sorrow. The passage we have selected closes with, again, the mention of Samuel growing up *"before the LORD."*

"The Lord Kills and Brings to Life"

Most of the passage before us describes how Eli's sons, under divine judgment and impulsion, choose and follow the way to self-destruction and death. The writer divides what he has to say on this depressing theme into three paragraphs. At the end of each of these, however, and in marked contrast to them, he places a series of short and cheerful and uplifting descriptions of how, while such destroying processes are ruthlessly working themselves out within one family circle, new life and hope are being created and nourished by God within another family circle, and indeed within the context of the life of Israel as a whole. *"The boy [Samuel]*,*"* we are reminded, *"remained to minister to the LORD, in the presence of the priest Eli"* (v. 11; cf. 3:1). We are then also informed that while Hannah herself was blessed with *"three sons and two daughters"* Samuel himself *"grew up in the presence of the LORD"* (v. 21). Later we are told that this was in every respect a healthy and promising development, that Samuel *"continued to grow both in stature and in favor with the LORD and with the people"* (v. 26).

This description of the boy growing up strong and good amidst infectious evil influences justifies Hannah's extraordinary and bold act of trusting little Samuel to the care of Eli. It illustrates for us, as is often done in the Bible, that even when some aspects of church life are polluted by unfaithfulness and error, God can still be at work honoring its ministry in his name. It underlines the word of assurance written by the Apostle John to his congregation also in evil days: "Little children, . . . the one who is in you is greater than the one who is in the world" (1 John 4:4). Samuel was an exceptional case, and it should in no way be quoted to encourage us to copy what Hannah did with her child. Still, it is good for us to know that the grace of God can keep and sanctify people forced to grow up, live, or work in an environment hostile to truth and goodness.

The writer of the narrative has another purpose in juxtaposing these vividly contrasting pictures. He wants to illustrate for us the central theme of Hannah's song of triumph: that the *"Lord kills and brings to life"* (2:6). God was there, in control of the darkness and death that visited Hophni and Phinehas, and he was there opening the mind of young Samuel to his truth and love. When Eli rebuked his two sons and warned them about the evil of their ways, the reason they took no heed is clearly given: *"They would not listen to the voice of their father; for it was the will of the Lord to kill them"* (v. 25). There is a great mystery here: Hophni and Phinehas by an act of personal self-determination choose their own evil road and actively pursue their course on it. They *"would not listen"!* Yet God himself also determines what is happening to them: *"It was the will of the Lord."*

We tend to underestimate the activity of God in controlling evil within human life and history. We imagine that he always plays the role of an idle spectator who permits many evil things to happen apart from his active control, intervening only now and then to ensure that affairs do not become entirely uncontrollable, and bringing judgment only on the final day of reckoning. This is not the picture the Bible gives us. God's hand rather is actively at work in the decay and degeneration that mark the careers of those who turn against him. He not only *decrees* that evil shall slay the wicked (Ps. 34:21); he directs and controls the evil by which the wicked are slain. We see him giving instructions to evil spirits and hardening human hearts in their wickedness (1 Sam. 16:14; 18:10; Exod. 7:13; 9:12, etc.). He makes the sword of the wicked enter their own heart (Ps. 37:15): "I am like maggots to Ephraim, and like rottenness to the house of Judah" (Hos. 5:12).

The Sins of the Young Men

It appears from the account given here that Eli's two sons had supervision of at least the preparation of the sacrifices that were then an important part of the ritual of Israel's worship. Though we find Eli alone presiding over the altar and holy place inside the sanctuary, we find that the servants of Hophni and Phinehas seem to have had the power to interfere freely with the cooking that was done for the sacrificial meals, which we can assume took place in the outer courts of the Temple then at Shiloh.

The two brothers apparently did not mix with the ordinary worshipers. We do not meet them in person in the Temple courts. We are allowed only to meet their servants. They appear to us therefore only as distant and shadowy figures who give instructions in the background, for they have no pastoral concern for their flock. Within their sphere of influence, however, they engage in the most sordid and greedy type of priestcraft. Even in those days the people at their feasts, some moved by true devotion, some by mere tradition or even superstition, brought costly offerings to the Temple. Hophni and Phinehas coveted for themselves the most choice of these. They sent their servants to do their business in their stead. They had invented for them a fork which, with the skill acquired after a little training, could probe, hook, and lift out of the pot exactly the joint required for their masters' table. They acted with the arrogance required for successful public relations in those rough days. When people protested, bullying tactics were used, and accusations of ignorance were thrown about. Priests knew better than people! If anyone still resisted, force was to be used. (See Additional Note at end of chapter.)

Their greed for good food was not their only lust. In spite of their pride and pastoral aloofness, they could not resist private meetings with some of the "holy" prostitutes who in those days surrounded and sometimes invaded the Temple courts in order to cater to the current fashion of mixing Baal worship with that of Yahweh. Talk went round, and even blind old Eli heard of it.

The writer, explaining why they became so despicable, gives a brief and trenchant diagnosis of the case. *"They had no regard for the Lord"* (v. 12). They were not entirely secular in their outlook; they believed superstitiously, for example, that the Ark possessed the power to scatter God's enemies in battle. They had some regard for religion and the part it could play in life. It was, however, for them a social and national religion without any pastoral dimension. No thought of a personal God or of a personal relationship with such a God ever entered their thought about what they were doing in the Temple. It never occurred to them that they might one day be called to give an account of their service, and nothing deterred them from the corrupting practices that marked their ministry. No hope of pleasing such a God ever encouraged them to faithfulness and goodness.

Moreover, *"They treated the offerings of the LORD with contempt"* (v. 17). These men had charge of the approach to God's altar. They were at the place where God's commandments were to be taught, where the infinite seriousness of every kind of human sin was to be exposed, and where blood was shed as a sign of the cost of putting things right with God. The moral health of God's people depended on what happened at that altar. Here the meaning of true repentance was meant to be taught; clean hands and pure heart were to be demanded of the worshiper. Here souls were meant to find forgiveness, and zeal for God's law was meant to be continually rekindled. Here, however, innocent, serious, and seeking people found their offering taken from them by the hands of cynical and careless priests, and they were at times sent back on their way baffled and offended.

At times during the history of Israel the priesthood failed badly by being overzealous in the exact performance of ritual and forgetful of the call to repentance. But here were two priests unconcerned about any aspect of their God-given task. They quenched the zeal of those who, inspired by the Spirit, had prepared themselves for costly sacrifice at the altar of God. They made what God offered seem cheap and easy to come by. By their flippancy and connivance as well as by their greed, they *"brought the LORD's sacrifice into general contempt"* (v. 17, NEB). People began to lose any vision they once may have had of God's holiness and grace, and life in Israel continued to lose its moral seriousness.

A Double-Minded Man

The conduct of Eli makes us ask a question of great importance to all of us who are engaged in the service of God. Why should a man who had so much that is likable and even godly about his life be so tragically ineffective as a public influence?

There were many noble traits in his character. Now and then, here and there, he tried to make a stand for a better way of life. God occasionally used him to bring blessing and good counsel to others. Hannah trusted him as if he were a worthy man. He was made the guardian and tutor of little Samuel! Yet under his administration, which lasted forty years, Israel's spiritual and moral life declined. In his later days, however hard he tried, he was unable to check the accelerating evil influence even of his own sons. When he heard they were having sex with the prostitutes around the Temple he merely deplored the spreading rumor, asked them why they did such things, and quoted a proverbial saying about the sins of priests being more serious than those of laymen.

It was late in his life that he was challenged seriously

about his failure. A *"man of God"* came to him in the Temple. We are not told exactly where this man came from. We read later of prophets who lived together in groups and prophesied under the influence of the Spirit. We read also of schools of prophets who flourished in the northern kingdom at the time of Elijah. Such groups may have been in their early development at this present period, and this prophet may have come from one of these. We cannot exclude the possibility that Hannah herself may have derived some encouragement from association with such people. The word of God spoken by this strange intruder ruthlessly exposed Eli himself as blameworthy for the greatest scandal of his time — for bringing the sacrifices of the altar into contempt. *"Why then look with greedy eye at my sacrifices and my offerings that I commanded, and honor your sons more than me by fattening yourselves on the choicest parts of every offering of my people Israel?"* (2:29).

In attributing the misuse of the offerings to Eli's *"greedy eye"* the nameless prophet is pointing to a defect at the heart of his relationship with God himself. His compromise had its roots deep within his soul. Certainly in many respects he was unlike his sons. Eli had a regard for God. As a religious man he had always at least tried to relate what he was doing to God. He had opened his mind and soul to divine influence. Yet at the same time deep down he had given scope and power for other influences, loyalties, and desires to take over his life and dictate his actions. His heart had never become united and completely dominated by the one single aim of living for the glory of God alone. He was like the "double-minded" man spoken of by St. James, weak in character and resolve, incapable of being motivated by any one great passion, and therefore "unstable in every way" (James 1:8). His case seems to be described for us in words of warning spoken by Jesus himself: "The light of the body is the eye: if therefore thine eye be single, thy whole body shall be full of light. But if thine eye be evil, thy whole body shall be full of darkness. If therefore the light that is in thee be darkness, how great is that darkness! No man can serve two masters: for either he will hate the one, and love the other; or else he will hold to the one, and despise the other. Ye cannot serve God and mammon" (Matt. 6:22-24, AV).

Therefore Eli was as weak in his ministry as he was weak in his character. It was because his sons knew how inwardly compromised he was, that they would not listen to anything he said. He was incapable of condemning the idolatry of his people with any passion. He was incapable of reflecting God's righteous anger in face of public outrage. Because he could not thus condemn obvious evil, he had no word adequate for his times. His defects and his failure illustrate for us a much-quoted saying from a popular religious work of the last century: "No heart is pure that is not passionate. No virtue is safe that is not enthusiastic."

All this is a reminder to us today as a church, of how the strength and effectiveness of our moral witness in any generation lies in the hearts of our own clergy and lay church leadership. The public image of the church certainly matters. We are right to insist that, as an institution, our investments and financial affairs be free from compromise with moral, social, and industrial evils. We cannot make any effective public protest against such evils if we are seen to profit from them financially. If such outward compromise enfeebles our witness, however, any inner compromise of heart is even more damaging. We cannot conduct an effective crusade against any vice we know to be destructive of home and society and of young life, if we ourselves do not genuinely abhor it and everything that stimulates and encourages it. Likewise we will not achieve clarity of thought on the controversial moral issues that continually come before us if we are thus "double-minded" (cf. James 4:8).

"Those Who Honor Me I Will Honor"

The sentence pronounced upon Eli and his house by the man of God must have broken the old man (cf. 2:10). Indeed, before it was given he could not have imagined it possible that such a word should have come from God. Years ago, in an act of pure grace and in a covenant that he and his family had held to be irrevocable, God had promised his forebears that they and their children would to all generations inherit the privilege of acting as high priests in this sanctuary: *"I promised that your family and the family of your ancestor should go in and out before me forever"* (v. 30a).

Eli had lived out his days as high priest, trusting in this word from a God who, he believed, never went back on what he had said. But now he seemed to hear the promise of God completely repudiated: *"Far be it from me; for those who honor me I will honor, and those who despise me shall be treated with contempt"* (v. 30b). God will not allow his name to be continually and methodically despised by those who claim to have

46

been elected to serve him, and who dare even to make that election the reason for the boldness to disobey him. Eli's sons absurdly and without any possible reason had substituted contempt and spite for trust and honor, and had thus rejected God's covenant with their family. They were to be slain, and the descendants of his house were to be impoverished (vv. 34, 36), and a *"faithful high priest"* was now to be raised up by God for himself, and *"I will build him a sure house, and he shall go in and out before my anointed one for ever"* (v. 35).

This word of God was fulfilled almost to the letter when Abiathar, who became the last survivor of the priestly line of Eli, was replaced in the priesthood by Zadok, under King Solomon (1 Kings 2:27; cf. 1 Sam. 22:17-20). From our New Testament standpoint, however, the promise about the *"faithful priest"* inevitably leads us directly to Christ himself, and to the new covenant that God made with Christ. He was the true high priest elected by God to give God due honor. How forcibly, clearly, and simply the words of the man of God summarize and help us understand what is required of us, and what promises are given to us, in the service of Christ! *"Those who honor me I will honor."* They are evangelical and relevant to all circumstances. They are a personal and gracious invitation in the first place to trust God, to become dependent on him, to receive his promises, and to open our lives to his grace. For we honor him most when we believe his promises and accept what he comes to us to give. We shall never be put to shame if we trust in him. Moreover, he has made us his brothers and sisters, his family, "a chosen race, a royal priesthood, a holy nation, God's own people."

We are each elected by him to "proclaim the mighty acts of him who called [us] out of darkness into his marvelous light" (1 Pet. 2:9).

A Vexing Question

It is possible that the condemnation, rather than the promise, uttered by this man of God might even be used against those of us who have been called to share this "royal priesthood" of the Lord Jesus Christ, and all the privileges of his fellowship and service. Can the covenant given to us by Christ be revoked in our case? Is it possible that we too can be rejected because instead of honor we have given contempt? It is a question sometimes seriously raised by anxious people who want to make their calling and election sure (2 Pet. 1:10) and who become troubled when they read about the "blasphemy against the Holy Spirit" which, Jesus said, can never be forgiven (Matt. 12:31-32).

In the tenth chapter of 1 Corinthians Paul reminds us that we must not underrate the moral thrust of the warnings given to us in these Old Testament stories. The temptations that people had then are the same as ours today, and we are in danger if we adopt the same attitude and take the same way as those who were then so severely punished. We must therefore take warning. Especially, if we feel sure that we are standing firm then let us beware, for we may fall. Yet even in this situation we can be confident, for God so loves us that he will provide a way of escape that we may be able to endure it (1 Cor. 10:1-13).

We are also reminded by Paul that the New Covenant is one now given to us "not in a written code but in the Spirit" (2 Cor. 3:6, RSV). Human nature proved itself too weak to fulfill even the gracious covenants made by God's mercy with men and women in the Old Testament. Therefore Christ came and fulfilled all these broken Old Testament covenants in our name and in our place, and his living and powerful Spirit within us enables us, even in spite of our human weakness, to will to honor God in the tasks he gives us to do. This is why the New Testament stresses the firmness, strength, and everlasting nature of the covenant that we have, in and with Christ. This is also why we are assured that God "never goes back upon his . . . call" (Rom. 11:29, Moffatt) and that once we belong to Christ no one is able to snatch us out of his hands (John 10:28-29). We have to remember that even under Old Testament conditions the sons of Eli were rejected only because by their contempt they repudiated God's loving approach to them. No trembling soul anxiously questioning whether he or she has despised the grace of God and therefore desperately seeking to please God can ever be said really to have despised it. Augustine's comment on the two thieves crucified beside Jesus is worth remembering: "One of the thieves was saved, therefore let us not despair: the other was damned, therefore let us not presume."

Additional Note on
the Priests' Portion of the Sacrifices (2:12-17)

Two aspects of Levitical law underlie the passage. First, the fat of each sacrifice was to be burnt as an offering to the Lord (Lev. 17:6; Num. 18:17), and it is clear that the worshipers were fully aware of this. Second, certain parts of the sacrifice were to be given to the priests as a form of stipend or income (Lev. 7:28-36; Deut. 18:3). The worshipers also knew this. However, *"while the meat was boiling,"* the avaricious priests' servants would seize whatever they could. Indeed, if they could get in early enough, they would demand choice cuts of meat *"before the fat was burned."* Their actions were clearly sacrilegious, showing total disregard of both the divine provision for the priests and also for the spiritual welfare of the worshipers.

CHAPTER 4

The Call of Samuel

1 Samuel 3:1-21

The Narrative

We are told the story of how, at a time when God's voice was seldom heard in Israel, Samuel one night heard himself called by name from the Ark. Thinking it was only Eli's voice, he ran to him, only to be told that he had not spoken. It was only after several such repeated happenings that Eli, realizing what was happening, told the boy to lie down and say, *"Speak, LORD, for your servant is listening."* The message he heard was of the forthcoming judgment on Eli and his sons. Samuel was afraid to speak of it to Eli in the morning until Eli himself gave the boy the courage to speak out and hide nothing. This was the beginning of Samuel's being acknowledged and listened to continually, over all Israel, as a prophet of the Lord.

"The Word of the LORD Was Rare"

The origin of everything that was most healthy and distinctive in the worship and culture of Israel was due to their hearing the word of God. From the days of Abraham, Isaac, and Jacob when they were one family, the word of God continually came to them, determining where they went and settled, inspiring them to action, and entering into their thoughts and plans. When they grew in number and became a group of families and tribes, they were held together because the same living God continued to speak to them. Moses at the burning bush heard the word of God calling him to leadership, and under its power and guidance came a great series of miracles — at the first Passover, at the Red Sea, and in the desert. The law was given; the promised land was entered and occupied.

When they were in the desert, under a covenant given by God, ritual began to be established that was to help them as a nation to hear the word of God from one generation to the next. A tabernacle, a tent of meeting, was constructed and set up to contain the Ark of the Covenant. When Moses went up to the tent of meeting to speak with the Lord, "he would hear the voice speaking to him from above the mercy seat that was on the ark of the covenant from between the two cherubim; thus it spoke to him" (Num. 7:89). Thus Moses was able always to pass on God's word of encouragement, warning, and guidance to the people, and they were continually kept in touch with God himself.

The view is sometimes put forward that the Temple at Shiloh was, or contained, the reinforced remnants of the same tent constructed by Moses. At any rate God saw to it that at the heart of the people's life there remained the place to which they could turn to hear the word that had given them everything that was precious in their life as a nation.

Now, however, a time had come in their history when the word of God was *"rare";* even around and within the tent of meeting at Shiloh a strange silence now prevailed. The members of the priesthood were most often dumb and distant from the people. When they did open their mouths they taught what seemed to be merely dead tradition or the foolish wisdom of their own minds mixed with pagan superstition. Certainly God kept up communication with his people in other ways than through the Temple services. Here and there in Israel by the grace of God people like the *"man of God"* mentioned earlier heard God speak and, as we have also seen, very occasionally even in the Temple a *"word"* came to people like Hannah and Elkanah, for instance. Yet the word was *"rare."*

The word was rare because people did not want to hear it. They had begun to resent many of the things God had said to prophets like Moses in laying down the strict laws that made them different from other nations and kept them apart. They had begun to want to have a bigger say in deciding their own customs, forms of worship, and destiny. In the ritual they wanted to become more like those other people around them who, instead of a word, had visible images that appealed to the senses. They wished that they could borrow ideas from the local Baal worship that gratified the natural instincts and desires.

We are meant to understand that God's silence at this

time in face of such resolute opposition to his word was deliberate and purposeful. When we survey the history of Israel throughout the whole Old Testament period we find that he seldom stopped appealing to them and calling people back to him. The prophets, for example, went on speaking his word even when it fell on deaf ears. Yet at times his patience seemed exhausted (cf. Ps. 18:26; Amos 8:11); on this occasion he simply turned away from his people for a time, withdrawing his word almost entirely from his Temple, and remaining distant. We can imagine that his conversation with us is out of love so sensitive that it tends to be silent when it finds that we do not even care to hear.

Empty Religion in a Silent Temple

Yet the ritual through which Israel's people were meant regularly to hear his word and come near to him was not neglected by the high priest and his young assistant. We are here given a picture of how little Samuel, girded with a linen ephod, assisted Eli in the task of ministry before the Lord. The little boy was no doubt given the most simple tasks of looking after the lights and keeping things clean. He was no doubt told about the history of the place and taught the stories of the people mentioned in the history and in the prayers he learned. He was told about the Ark, about Moses' tent, and warned to preserve its holiness. Was he not also warned not to go the way of Eli's own sons, and to ward off the bad women who were apt to intrude especially when they were drunk? It is implied in the account we have of the daily ritual that, nightly, when the lamp of God was flickering and about to go out, they lay down each in his own place, Samuel having been allocated one very near the Ark of God. Scholars suggest that even their act of lying down before the lamp had gone out may have been an important part of the traditional ritual that Eli automatically followed, and taught to Samuel. As they lay down at this particular time it was customary for the priests to adopt a listening posture so that they could hear the voice of the Lord as Moses had done, if it came. It was such a long time since any word had come even to him that Eli had obviously put out of his mind any expectation of its ever occurring again. Little Samuel had merely been taught to act in this way without any inkling of what it meant. The ritual to both of them was merely a priestly way of going to sleep, as they actually did, night after night — at the very hour when they should have been alert to listen for the word of God!

Our own traditional form of worship today, especially if we belong to the Reformed tradition, implies that we also, as we engage in the ritual of our divine service together, should also hear the living voice of God to which Samuel and Eli should have been alert. The appeal is made before the reading of each Scripture: "Hear the Word of God." The sermon is meant to be preached with one chief aim in mind: that through the exposition and repetition of the text, the hearers may be pointed to the living Lord himself, may be confronted by him and hear him speaking to them. Jesus, indeed, implied in his teaching that through the voice of an earthly pastor, his own sheep within the gathered congregation would hear his own voice (John 10:27).

Can it be that the writer of this narrative had his finger on exactly our chief church problem: that *the word of the Lord is rare?* We find our worship lacking because it does not really give us what it promises. No voice breaks through to us from beyond our everyday world. Holy Scripture has become to many of us merely a book of ancient literature which, as our scholars so often tell us, requires to be heard with caution and interpreted under the guidance of an expert in theology and ancient languages, well trained to instruct us in the correct teaching. The sermon comes through to us as the word of man — interesting, well prepared, even a challenging and elevating aspect of timeless truth, yet a word of man (cf. 1 Thess. 2:13). In pastoral counseling, which is meant to accompany the preaching, the dynamics are often purely psychological, and everything takes place on an earthly level. The voice that was heard by Abraham, Moses, and the prophets, and that later on showed its power at the Lake of Galilee, the voice that raised Lazarus from the dead, healed diseases, and stilled the storm does not seem to be heard.

The far-reaching spiritual and moral effects of our failure to hear the word of God are indicated for us in the writer's comment on the plight of those who frequented the silent Temple: *"no vision was granted"* (v. 1, NEB). They had nothing more to lift their minds to than their own bitter life-and-death struggle to survive in the harsh natural conditions around them and the threats and ravages of enemy invaders. They had no hope of any light from beyond ever illuminating the darkness that fringed their life, nothing to relieve them when the problems and pressures of life became unbearable or when disease or death deprived them of their earthly joy and hope. The inevitable happened. "Where there is no revelation, the people cast off restraint" (Prov. 29:18, NIV).

We are not far today from this picture of a people turning to a permissiveness that destroys the basis even of decent living, and we do not need to look far among friends and associates to meet those who are "troubled and heavy laden" because life as they find it is empty of meaning and it asks for much more than it seems to give. In the time of the great financial depression of the 1930s, which was also for many a time of spiritual depression, there was an editorial in the American journal *Fortune* that was much quoted at the time of its appearance in 1939. It appealed to the church to speak in a voice in which the laity would hear something that was more than an echo of their own. "Unless we hear such a voice, men of this generation will sink into the spiral of depression about which economists speak. There is only one way out of the spiral. The way out is the sound of a voice, not our voice, but a voice coming from something beyond ourselves in the existence of which we cannot disbelieve. It is the earthly task of pastors to hear this voice and to tell us what it says. If they cannot hear it or if they fail to tell us, we as laymen are utterly lost."

The Beginning of a Friendship

The familiar form of the conversation entered during this call is one of its important features. No vision or visible sign was given to Samuel along with the spoken word. In this respect the story of Samuel's call differs from the stories of other calls in the Bible. Moses saw a burning bush. Isaiah and Ezekiel and Jacob saw visions of the heavens open before them. Jeremiah's call was confirmed by things he was able to see with his eyes. With Samuel it was all by the voice, the tone of which was familiar and human. It sounded at first so gentle and unpretentious that Samuel could not believe it to be the voice of the Lord. Had he not often heard accounts of how God thundered when he spoke so awesomely that the people of Israel had begged him no longer to speak directly to them, but to give his messages through Moses? Yet here he was speaking directly, yet gently and appealingly, in the kind of voice that Eli used to use when he wanted to draw his attention, to tell him things that were interesting, or to get him to do some work he had for him. It echoed fondly the name his mother had given him when she was so full of hope that he would become a great servant of the Lord, and the call was so patiently and gently repeated when he failed at first to guess who was speaking.

The circumstances to which God had subjected him in his early youth had inured him to loneliness, and had made him able to bear it. And now God himself had broken in as if he wanted to heal the sometimes sore emptiness. From this moment everything in his mind about life and about God underwent a complete transformation. The story tells us (v. 7) that though he had of course known *about* God, Samuel had not yet had the least personal encounter with him. Now the friendship began, and began wonderfully. For the first time in his life he began to understand what it meant that the Lord of the whole earth could call Abraham "my friend" (2 Chron. 20:7; Isa. 41:8)!

Here for him now began the relationship that gave him the personal motive for offering himself as the full sacrifice that had been foreshadowed when his mother *"lent him to the* Lord." Here began the growing experience of God's presence that later gave him the courage and strength to bear all the reproach and rejection that came when his prophetic suffering became intensely hard.

When we read today about all that happened to Samuel — the beginning of an inseparable friendship; the calling of a name; the approach to a lonely boy from one who had cared about him even before his birth, and who knew everything about him that there was to be known; the voice human and familiar, impelling yet appealing — are we not very near to the world we read of in the Gospels — the world of Jesus and his disciples? Was not his ideal for the relationship between them and himself that of friendship? Did that friendship not grow from quiet and undemonstrative beginnings to become an unfailing source of peace and faith in God? Did Jesus not even at the beginning call to them by their names, and before he was introduced to them did he not give them at times new names to live up to? Were they not aware even at the beginning that he knew each of them better than they knew themselves? And was his voice, which to them was also the voice of God, not also human and familiar, impelling yet appealing? And did he not call them to himself so that he might send them out to serve and preach?

Here again we are confronted with the mystery that the one whom many of them could remember as he was in Galilee and Jerusalem was the same one who had already been there so often in the life of the people of God, speaking there, as he had spoken when in the flesh, with the same love, persuasiveness, and power as he will ever have.

Samuel's Early Ministry

Samuel was given a good beginning to his career as a prophet. There was to come a long period during which he was not seriously listened to by the people he was sent to serve; but at first everything did go well. So *"as Samuel grew up, the LORD was with him and let none of his words fall to the ground"* (v. 19).

That *none* of Samuel's words fell to the ground could mean, as the New English Bible translates it: that *"none of his words went unfulfilled."* No prophecy Samuel made about things that were going to happen ever proved false. But in view of Jesus' teaching in the parables of the sower, the seed, and the soils, we would be justified in also giving it the meaning that none of his words went unheeded, or failed to find an entrance into the hearts and minds of hearers. His preaching, in other words, was not in vain. There was no empty rhetoric evaporating in the air. His message was such that people were forced to face the issues he raised.

His reputation spread. *"And all Israel from Dan to Beersheba knew that Samuel was a trustworthy prophet of the LORD"* (v. 20). He may have traveled up and down the whole country, being in demand everywhere, or it may be that people who made pilgrimages to Shiloh heard his word and took news with them.

Samuel's friendship with God, we are told, was continually renewed, as it were day by day. *"The LORD continued to appear at Shiloh, for the LORD revealed himself to Samuel at Shiloh by the word of the LORD"* (v. 21). The word of God kept coming to him. New aspects of its truth were being unfolded to his mind, and his vision was enlarged. He grew in understanding of what had been previously said so that his preaching always had fresh content and inspiration. Moreover, precisely because he kept in touch with the living Lord and his word, he was able to meet the pressing and varied needs of whoever came, weary and humble to hear what God had to say. Like a true servant of God, "morning by morning" God met him and "waken[ed] his ear to listen as those who are taught" so that he could "know how to sustain the weary with a word" (Isa. 50:4).

Though Eli was so slow at first to understand what was happening, we must not underestimate the important part he was finally given to play in helping Samuel to understand what was happening and to find his way. He helped the youngster not only to hear the word. He also impressed his mind with the importance of speaking exactly what he heard, without gloss or amendment. God, he knew, had laid down the law for the prophet: "I will put my words in the mouth of the prophet, who shall speak to them everything that I command" (Deut. 18:18). In the morning he recognized Samuel's hesitancy and confusion before him, guessed the cause of his tension, and spoke to him a word that Samuel must have felt to be from God too. *"Samuel, my son. What was it that he told you? Do not hide it from me. May God do so to you and more also, if you hide anything from me of all that he told you"* (vv. 16-17).

How relevant this word for today! We have become too expert at shielding ourselves from the full impact of the Word of God upon us by deliberately ignoring what we do not wish to hear. We often tend to do this not simply as individuals, but within the common life we share with others in the church. Each generation of church people tends to select from the Bible only what it wants to hear — whatever gives it comfort and does not too much disturb its ways of thinking and acting. The result is that we entrench ourselves in a world of partial theological, biblical, and moral insights, and we do not want to be disturbed by other aspects of biblical truth that have been neglected or rejected in the formation of our way of life and thinking.

It would be unjust to move on without one final word in praise of Eli. He had by this time already heard himself condemned by the *"man of God"* (2:27-36) and had accepted it with contrition. When now he heard from Samuel that there was no way he could avoid the judgment that had already been pronounced, then at that very moment he acknowledged God's goodness and gave glory to him in accepting his own condemnation. He ceased pleading for mercy because God himself had forbidden it. He offered himself as a sacrifice to be slain by God's word. *"It is the LORD; let him do what seems good to him."* We can compare him with Abraham, facing certainly a different kind of word but also accepting it without reserve and giving glory to God by believing it. Abraham "believed the LORD; and the LORD reckoned it to him as righteousness" (Gen. 15:6).

We can think of words spoken by saintly King Hezekiah in the midst of his affliction. "But what can I say? For he has spoken to me, and he himself has done it" (Isa. 38:15). When we read, later, about Eli at the hour of his death, we find ourselves appalled by the isolation and sheer misery with which he was then visited. Men reap what they sow! Here, however, we have a sign that there is at least an eternal hope even in face of judgment if there is true contrition and submission to the word of God.

It was an encouraging start. Samuel for a while was spared the humiliation of being publicly neglected. No doubt he experienced the gathering round him of a small congregation of those whose lives had begun to be opened to God as his own had been. Yet he was soon to discover that Israel's response as a nation was superficial. The acknowledgment that there was a genuine prophet in their midst did not mean that in any way their leadership began to respond with heart and will to his teaching. Samuel had to learn to wait.

CHAPTER 5

Aphek and Its Aftermath

1 Samuel 4:1-22

The Narrative

A war that broke out between Israel and the Philistines ended with a disastrous defeat. When the elders of Israel reviewed the shameful situation they decided to return the attack. This time they wisely would make certain that God would give them victory by taking the Ark with the two sons of Eli along with them on the field. Disaster ensued. The Ark was captured and the priests were killed. We then read the touching accounts of how the news was received, first by Eli and then by the wife of Phinehas who heard it while she was in labor with their child.

Israel Disturbed and Tested

"Israel went out to battle against [the Philistines]" (v. 1). Suddenly events took an unexpected turn. The movement of renewal

that had seemed so promising was interrupted. The Philistines threatened and war broke out. A disaster occurred from which it took Israel twenty years fully to recover.

When Israel entered the promised land under the leadership of Joshua they were enabled here and there to obtain a firm foothold through a series of remarkable victories, and in certain areas a process of gradual takeover began. But they had for generations to struggle against both the native peoples and invaders from abroad who challenged their claim to the territory. The most menacing of all these invaders were the Philistines, who had a long-established tradition of fighting and war, were vastly superior in military skills, and had much better weapons.

The hostility between the two peoples arose not simply because each wanted to dominate the same territory, but because they were so opposed to each other in religious outlook and culture.

In religion, the policy of the Philistines was simply to adopt as their own whatever gods were regarded by the previous inhabitants as native to that soil. They had therefore, since landing in Canaan, built their temples to the local Baal gods, and centered their religious devotion on them. The duty and aim of the Israelites, wherever they settled, however, was laid down by Moses: "break down their altars, smash their pillars, hew down their sacred poles, and burn their idols with fire" (Deut. 7:5).

In an important passage in the book of Judges, the Philistines are given a prominent place in the list of peoples whom God is said to have left in Canaan so that he might "test" Israel by them (Judg. 3:1).

One of the purposes of this "testing" was to be that the generations of the people of Israel might discover God's readiness to help them in time of war. When God decided to save the world's history from a disastrous future, he decided to save it by creating a special people Israel, whose history in the midst of other nations would find its consummation in One who was to be the Savior of the world through his life, teaching, and death. God's people therefore had to be willing to be involved in war. Indeed they had to be prepared to face any kind of struggle demanded from them in the midst of earth's dangers and threats, in order to fulfill God's great purpose for them as a nation. Yet in the midst of such history they were never to trust in or take pride in their weapons or military skill. Their trust must be only in God. At the heart of one of their great psalms was the prayer: "scatter the peoples who delight in war" (Ps. 68:30).

A second purpose of the testing was "to know whether Israel would obey the commandments of the LORD, which he commanded their ancestors by Moses" (Judg. 3:4). God wanted to find out whether they were prepared continually to resist the temptation to religious and moral compromise with those who were threatening them. It was fitting therefore that as the word began to spread through Israel under Samuel, and as people began to respond to his ministry, God should want to test what was taking place. If the movement towards God was genuine, it would be revealed in their reactions to the Philistine army. Would they now genuinely search their hearts and put away what had separated them from God? Would they pray for his help, seek his guidance, and put their trust in his power alone? Only in the midst of such crisis could the answers to such questions be decisively given.

Evasion

The war did not open auspiciously. During a first disastrous battle their army was *"put . . . to rout."* Their troops, lacking morale and courage, had fled before the enemy, and it is significant that we read beforehand of no attempt by their leaders even to pray. The crucial test of Israel's faith, however, came after this defeat when their elders met in council and began to raise the important religious question: *"Why has the LORD put us to rout today before the Philistines?"* (v. 3).

Their history could have taught them there and then clearly what was to be done — turn to the Lord in repentance and faith, to wait on him for his guidance, and to obey his word. Instead, they thought of the Ark, their religious treasure. It was a wooden box containing the stone tablets on which the Ten Commandments were written. Because of this it was called the Ark of the Covenant. It had been placed by Moses in the tabernacle, and there it was also regarded as a sign of God's presence. Moses had turned towards it in order to hear the word of God. When the people were journeying through the desert the Ark was carried in a prominent place in their midst. When it was lifted up to take the lead on any dangerous advance they would sing: "Arise, O LORD, and let your enemies be scattered." Under Joshua, the Ark at the command of God was carried by the priests into the Jordan to divide the waters so that the rest of Israel was able to cross dry shod. Moreover, it was often carried in front of them as a sign that God was leading them on their pilgrimage (Josh. 3:1-13).

Why not make God relive with them those old histories? Was not God there in the Temple and where the Ark was — and had he not recently at times spoken to Samuel in its presence? If they now took the Ark into battle would this not mean that they would inevitably have God on their side against the enemy? They forgot God's hatred of human presumption and pride, how he punished those who dared to try to manipulate him and challenge him to do their will. They convinced themselves, reasoning from a few texts and a few simple facts, that with the Ark at their disposal they had God at their disposal. He would protect them because he was pledged to protect the Ark. *"Let us bring the ark of the covenant of the* Lord *here from Shiloh, so that he may come among us and save us from the power of our enemies"* (v. 3).

Superficially, of course, they did pay some heed to their religious tradition and to what Samuel was saying. They asked pious questions, they consulted passages from their scriptures, and as Samuel himself must have done at this time, they laid great stress on the fact that the Lord of their history loved to make his presence known where the Ark was. But they took from the word of God that had come to them only what they could distort and assimilate to their own perverse way of thinking, and they rejected what they did not like. They were determined to try to solve their religious problems in their own way. They had for years felt comfortable with a superstitious form of false religion like that found among the heathen cults of their neighbors in

Canaan. These people had gods who were easily manipulated, who could be forced into action by the performance of humanly devised ritual. It was their belief that where you had an idol or even a religious symbol then you had the god who belonged to the symbol. The elders of Israel wanted this kind of religion — a religion that demanded of them no more effort than the mechanical performance of a prescribed ritual. They wanted to avoid becoming involved in a religion that demanded the moral change and radical repentance emphasized by the traditional prophets. Therefore they came back to the Ark rather than to the Lord. They forgot that God is a person, independent, free, holy, loving, and demanding. They no longer dared to think of him in such a way. They could not face up to the moral change demanded by an honest and open approach to and encounter with one who was holy. Therefore they made him, in their thinking, merely an impersonal influence to be manipulated and controlled and somehow bound up with the objects through which he had chosen in his grace to bless his people.

Folly upon Folly

God therefore allowed Israel to abandon themselves completely to their folly, and they allowed themselves to be deluded. They felt that the religious enthusiasm which the Ark inspired was itself the divine presence. Their emotion told them that God himself was with them, and their hearts took fresh courage. They felt themselves to be really now on the verge of the national renewal for which Samuel had been calling. Unprepared and unfit, they allowed themselves to be carried forward into battle.

We are meant to notice the touch of irony that runs through the whole account of the affair. Their pious desire to copy their forefathers in the faith brought to their memory that when Joshua with the Ark faced Jericho, the walls had fallen and the enemy had been routed after the great shout that had accompanied the blast on the trumpets. They were led therefore as they came face to face with the Philistine host to give *"a mighty shout, so that the earth resounded"* (v. 5). The shout was confidently intended to inspire the Philistines with terror, and to force them to break ranks and take flight. Instead, it inspired them with valor. Everything that happened confounded expectation and explanation. *"Woe to us!"* cried the enemy (v. 7), and in their desperate fear, instead of fleeing they rallied. *"Who can deliver us from the power of these mighty gods?"* they cried. *"These are the gods who struck the Egyptians with every sort of plague in the wilderness. Take courage, O Philistines . . . and fight"* (vv. 8-9). So *"the Philistines fought"* (v. 10). It was as if Israel had unwittingly prepared a trap for their own self-destruction and then walked into it. They fled from the battle, and many were slaughtered as they ran to their homes (v. 10). It became a proverbial saying in Israel, "He takes the wise in their own craftiness" (Job 5:13).

The spirit of folly is shown in many stories of the Bible to take many forms as it leads people on a path of self-destruction and inspires them inevitably towards their doom. Sometimes as with Absalom it takes the form of uncontrollable vanity and ambition. Sometimes as with Nabal the Carmelite it manifests itself in simple pigheaded and obstinate dislike of normal, decent people (1 Sam. 25). Sometimes as with the fool in Christ's parable it becomes the mad business of accumulating and controlling more and more money at the cost of God's friendship and everything else that is tender and more valuable in human life. In the book of Proverbs we have the story of the young man blindly and inevitably led on by sexual lust to his own death. "There is a way that seems right to a person, but its end is the way to death" (Prov. 7:6-27; 14:12; 16:2). In this particular story the folly takes a very different form but the consequences are no less disastrous. Here we have the folly of men who have deliberately blinded themselves to the truth of God and deserted his revelation, gripped and controlled by their own perverse ideas of God and his ways. The way they took and the way God took with them is trenchantly described by St. Paul: "For though they knew God, they did not honor him as God or give thanks to him, but they became futile in their thinking, and their senseless minds were darkened" (Rom. 1:21). The way God dealt with them is also described by the Apostle: "since they did not see fit to acknowledge God, God gave them up to a debased mind" (Rom. 1:28).

The News Comes Home — Eli

The news of the disaster was brought to the homesteads around Shiloh by a man of Benjamin who *"ran from the battle line, and came to Shiloh the same day, with his clothes torn and with earth upon his head"* (v. 12). We are given two dramatic pictures of how it was received.

When Eli heard the *"the sound of the outcry"* around him as the news traveled from home to home (v. 14), he was already trembling. He had not recovered from the shock given to him when Hophni, Phinehas, and their fellows came, and in their fit of madness violated the holy place which he had tried so zealously all his life to guard, and seized the Ark. His protests had not been listened to, and he had been left alone in the desecrated sanctuary — bewildered that God himself had let it happen and wondering why his sons already under the sentence of death had escaped that moment with their lives. They had left him alone, unattended, in the deserted and empty place and, not bearing to remain there, though blind, he had groped his way to the roadside and had sat down on a seat. His first concern and chief task had always been the guardianship of the Ark — the protection of its sanctity. In spite of the faults that now he knew only too well to have marred his life, he had tried to do this one thing faithfully. To him the Ark had always been the pledge of God's goodness and love for Israel, and his experience on that night when young Samuel was called to be a prophet had brought back to him a fresh sense of the very grace and holiness it symbolized. Could Israel, God's people, have any future at all now that they had so recklessly and wantonly abused it? He thought of his sons. He had known that they were doomed, but he had never imagined that they would die so deserving of God's anger.

As he looked back over his life, his conscience awakened

by the word of God greatly troubled him. He had been in a key position and by being faithful years ago he might have prevented this catastrophe! But nothing he could even begin to do now could put anything around him right. His situation helps us to understand what Jesus meant when he spoke about a soul becoming "lost" — overwhelmed and without understanding of the events around him, apparently overtaken entirely by the sins of the past. The form of his tragic death brings to our mind an image of what he inwardly felt about himself and his life. It gives us a picture of the inward brokenness of the man's spirit, of his bitter loneliness of soul, and of his blindness to any vision that might bring hope. Blind and alone he *"fell over backward from his seat by the side of the gate; and his neck was broken and he died, for he was an old man, and heavy"* (v. 18).

At this point we are asked to reflect on the fact that *"he had judged Israel forty years"* (v. 18). Perhaps the writer means us to read this as a devastating comment on the kind of ruler with which people are sometimes saddled — even the people of God! — for his death revealed something of his character even as a ruler. Perhaps it is simply a warning that even those in the highest position must in the end come to dust, some of them in such a way as this, if they fail to seek first the kingdom of God.

The News Comes Home — Phinehas' Wife

The second picture we are given here, that of Phinehas' wife hearing the news, reminds us of Jeremiah's harrowing descriptions of what war can do, especially when its effects reach the homes and the women of the land:

> Hear, O women, the word of the LORD,
>> and let your ears receive the word of his mouth;
> teach your daughters a dirge,
>> and each to her neighbor a lament.
> "Death has come up into our windows,
>> it has entered our palaces,
> to cut off the children from the streets
>> and the young men from the squares."
> Speak! Thus says the LORD:
> "Human corpses shall fall
>> like dung upon the open field,
> like sheaves behind the reaper,
>> and none shall gather them."
>> (Jer. 9:20-22; cf. 9:17-19; 10:17-21)

It reminds us, too, of Jesus' own heart-rending warning to us of what can happen in the life of people who choose to neglect warnings, and who are taken unawares in the midst of the upheavals that will accompany the coming of his kingdom: "Woe to those who are pregnant and to those who are nursing infants in those days!" (Mark 13:17)

As we read this account of the pain and mental desolation of this poor woman in giving birth to her child under such harrowing circumstances, we are meant to contrast this chapter's end with its beginning. We are meant to remember the exultant confidence of the elders of Israel as they plunged their people into this second bloody battle. It was to be a glorious and quick war in the name of the Lord. Here at the end of the chapter we are given a picture of the bitterness, desolation, and shame that so often in history have visited the homes and the women of a community because the men who decided their affairs were irresponsible. Here we are shown how the sins of a husband are visited upon his wife, how the sins of the fathers are visited upon the children, how a heritage built up by generations of toil and faith can be ruthlessly squandered in a moment or two.

The writer intends to invoke both our sympathy and our admiration for this poor woman, the wife of Phinehas. She was obviously deeply religious; she cared for her father-in-law Eli, the news of whose death helped to bring her too to her death. Like him her faith in God and Israel was somehow linked up with the Ark. Before the disaster fell she would have been justified in confidently looking forward to what the future held both for herself and for the child in her womb — especially if he were a boy! He would become the custodian of the Ark of God and would serve all his days in the Temple. He would rule in Israel. The picture we have of her here justifies us in thinking of her as innocent of the corruption that prevailed there in God's courts. She was proud to think of her husband as one great in God's sight. Had she not been thrilled to watch him going out in the midst of the army that was to save Israel from its enemies?

On hearing the news, the whole background of her life and hope suddenly collapsed. When she heard the news, *"her labor suddenly began and she crouched down and was delivered"* (v. 19, NEB). The midwives tried to encourage her to live, telling her that God had blessed her with a son. But for her now one thought alone possessed her mind and filled it with utter darkness, and brought about her death. Since the Ark had been taken, God had surely deserted his people and had gone back on all his promises. There was nothing left to live for. No future worth struggling for — even for her child. The glory had departed from Israel — and from life itself.

One thing we must admire in her. Though her mind was mistaken about many things she was clear-sighted about one great central issue. She shared the faith of Abraham, Isaac, and Jacob that the whole future of human history and indeed of existence on this earth depended on the glory that God had given and would again give to his people Israel. That belief had been the light by which she lived. When to her it appeared to have been shattered, all life was dark and comfortless.

There can be little doubt that we are meant by the writer to compare her with Hannah. How near indeed they were to each other! Each shared the same belief about the destiny of her nation and the future of world history. Each frequented the same Temple. Each respected and trusted Eli. Each is introduced to us by the writer as passing through intense suffering. Each gave conception to a child destined, they believed, to serve the people of God — and yet how distant each was from the other and how great the contrast between them!

For Hannah everything was open to hope. The last words we hear from her are a song of joy about the glory that she believed was soon to come to Israel. Her years of agony had been fruitful. Her child, she was certain, would be great in the sight of the Lord. She saw a new age about to begin within the life of Israel. She believed it would come about because she was in touch with and believed in the kingdom of God. "We do not lose heart," said Paul, "because we look not at what can be seen but at what cannot be seen; for what can be seen is temporary, but what cannot be seen is eternal" (2 Cor. 4:16, 18). For Phinehas' wife there was only the world around her, the world of Hophni and Phinehas — a world under condemnation, and now passing away under the judgment of God. The glory had departed from Israel. Her agony was fruitless. She had borne a child for a wasted empty inheritance.

"Two women will be grinding meal together," said Jesus. "One will be taken and one will be left" (Matt. 24:41). There are two different kinds of grief, said Paul (2 Cor. 7:10), a "godly grief" that in the end "brings no regret" and a "worldly grief" that "produces death." There are two different foundations upon which people can toil to build, even with devoted lifelong zest, skill, and energy, and yet only when the day of testing comes are the deep and hidden differences in foundation revealed (Matt. 7:24-27).

New Testament Hope

The Old Testament should direct our thoughts to the New, not always, however, to find what fulfills its prophecies and its aspiration, but also to find there, in contrast, what reveals the answer to our present need. When we read of Eli in his desperate anxiety sitting at the roadside in his blindness waiting for news, can our thoughts not turn to a man in the New Testament, also blind and with as little to live for as Eli, he too sitting by the roadside? He was begging and asking passersby for news. But Jesus came his way — "He regained his sight and followed him, glorifying God" (Luke 18:43). When we read of Eli in his final moment of utter despair and death, are we not meant also to think of the dying thief on the cross? One thing we do know about Eli is that he accepted without murmur the judgment of God that had been pronounced on his family. We are meant to honor him for this. King Saul when he was told, like Eli, that God had rejected him and that his house would not succeed to the kingship, became rebellious, bitter, and jealous. Saul then tried to kill the chosen David. There was not a trace of rebellion or bitterness in Eli. Saul stands out in the biblical story like the dying thief who railed at Jesus and taunted him. Does Eli in contrast not stand out like the one who sought and found mercy? Though he could not now put anything around him right, is it not possible that by his faith and God's mercy he put himself right? (See Luke 23:39-43.)

From this tragic Old Testament passage our thoughts turn to Mary the mother of Jesus: "she gave birth to her firstborn son and wrapped him in bands of cloth, and laid him in a manger . . . and he was called Jesus . . . and suddenly there was . . . a multitude of the heavenly host, praising God and saying, 'Glory to God in the highest heaven, and on earth peace among those whom he favors!'" (Luke 2:7, 21, 13-14). Of course she is the Hannah of the New Testament. She embodies and perfects everything that was there in the mother of Samuel. Here is the place in the future towards which, unknown to herself, Hannah's mind was searching when she prayed for a son.

If only Phinehas' wife had had even a small measure of the vision and hope of Hannah, she, too, would have seen that the glory of God could never depart from Israel. Here at the beginning of the New Testament is the birth, the influence of which is meant to banish from human life all the darkness that hemmed in the mind and vision of this poor tragic soul. Here is what can make all human toil and agony from now on fruitful.

CHAPTER 6

The Ark among the Philistines

1 Samuel 5:1–6:15

The Narrative

The Ark, we read, in its captivity brought fear and panic wherever it was taken. When it was put in the temple of their god Dagon, the morning light revealed that the pagan idols of the false gods around it were during the first night flattened, and the next night smashed. When it was then taken from city to city its presence was marked by unusual diseases and plagues. The lords of the Philistines, responding to the fear of the people, had to find a suitable way of sending it back. Their own magicians suggested that they appease the God of Israel by the gift in an accompanying box of models in gold of mice and tumors. As a difficult test of God's power, they suggested that the Ark and these gifts should be placed in a new cart harnessed to two milking cows forcibly separated from calves. The Lord miraculously responded to the challenge by inspiring the cows to forsake their calves and head towards Israel, without human guidance. We have a touching picture of the arrival of the Ark at the field of a certain Joshua at Bethshemesh, the person most likely to recognize the greatness of the occasion and give it a worthy reception.

The Crisis and the Shame

After Aphek, many in Israel were being tempted to ask critical questions. God had promised a future full of blessing, and now they were facing years of direct slavery under a ruthless enemy, economic disaster, and broken homes, with their Temple and official priesthood destroyed, the leaders discredited. Some were facing, with what they felt justifiable bitterness, many questions that never before had entered their minds. Did the Ark in the hands of the Philistines not mean that God had now cast them off, that his plan for them was irrevocably finished, and that any call for further repentance from a preacher like Samuel was to no purpose? Did the Ark in the hands of the Philistines not mean that they had been deceived about their God? Had they not now incontestable proof that the Baal gods of the Philistines were more powerful than the Lord? Moreover, did this mean that Baal religion was as good, if not even better than the religion taught by Moses? Might not their great leader have been wrong in some of the most important points in their creed?

The nations around Israel had been continually impressed by the way this people had been at times miraculously protected and helped when they were in hopeless danger, and there had been a growing respect for their unique faith and way of life, and for the name of their God. But now it seemed to the Philistines that such fears and questions about *"these mighty gods"* (cf. 4:8) who had powerfully protected this small nation and brought them out of Egypt were now groundless. The Ark that had terrified them had failed to inspire its own worshipers with the courage even to stand and fight. It was simply a box with little to it! Now suddenly the reputation of the God of the whole earth seems to be at stake among the nations, and we ourselves have to face the question: Did God himself plan, or even expect to face, such a situation?

The Humiliation and Patience of God

One of the psalmists dwells on this particular incident and asks us to meditate especially on the burden of shame and anger that God himself had to bear as he faced and overcame this crisis in his dealings with his people. He asks us to think of what it meant for him among the nations to have his Ark debased, deserted, defiled, and humiliated (see Ps. 78:60, 61, 64).

It was surrendered without a struggle! Only Philistines fought, and Israel "fled, everyone to his home" (4:10). It was as if the God of Israel himself in that instant was deserted entirely by those he looked to for a sign of loyalty. Through this symbol of his presence he had given his people unfailing and forgiving comfort, love, and encouragement from generation to generation, had led them through the desert into the promised land, and had pledged them future blessing and glory. Yet not one was found to fight for it when it seemed for a moment to hold no magic power to fight for them.

Humiliation followed desertion. God watched and saw the symbol of his "power" and his "glory" (Ps. 78:61) gaped at by the ignorant, prodded and examined by the curious. Like all the captive gods of defeated enemies, it too was taken in procession round their cities and set up for public display in the temples. Its final fate would be decided when the wise men, the Philistine magicians and kings, came together in council. Perhaps it could be bartered for political concession. Perhaps it could become a valuable museum piece.

Sovereignty in Crisis

As we read through the story in this and the following chapter we are meant primarily to notice the sheer sovereignty and adaptability with which God faced this critical situation. We have to note the ease and deftness with which he manipulated every seemingly casual or unforeseen aspect of the emergency as it arose before him without even a trace of embarrassment.

The story is told with restraint and simplicity. No time was lost. God inspired the Philistines themselves to set the stage for what was to be done, and they produced exactly the conditions he needed. The Ark was put alongside their idol

Dagon in their temple at Ashdod. They thought they were putting the finishing touches to the humiliation of the God of Israel. Though they did not know it, they were setting a trap into which their own god would fall. The doors were shut and all was left quiet for the night. And, as if in the hours of darkness a contest in heaven had taken place, there in the morning his priests and devotees found Dagon flat on his face! At first they explained it satisfactorily to themselves — weak cement, perhaps, poor workmanship when the top-heavy idol was set up on its base! They put it right and made it secure. But next night Dagon was again dislodged before the Ark of the Lord, with head and hands cut off and lying beside his platform. Thus by two deftly executed signs, one after the other, God said and did everything that should have been required — had the minds of the enemy been open to the message!

Nothing more need have been done or said anywhere among the Philistines to restore God's name and honor. It was a repetition of what had happened in Egypt. There the sun and the Nile represented for the Egyptian the divine sources of their well-being and life. There God had entered conflict with both. The sun had been turned to darkness and the life-giving power of the river had been destroyed. Here in Ashdod the Lord had shown his power against the gods of the Philistines as he had against the gods of Egypt (Exod. 12:12).

We are meant to notice the gentleness of his approach to the whole task of rescuing the Ark. In the long run the Philistines themselves had to be hurt. It was only after their cities were visited by plague that they began to cry out, *"Send away the ark of the God of Israel, and let it return to its own place, that it may not kill us and our people"* (5:11). But God tried persuasion before he resorted to such force. He was concerned not to destroy but to save life. He wanted to destroy only their idols. In the end, even though the people were terror-struck, their leaders were well aware of what had happened within the temple of Dagon. They had to face the evidence honestly and calmly, and to acknowledge the power of the Lord.

As we read through the story in the light of what is said in Psalm 78 (vv. 56-62), we are meant also to notice that within this unique salvation history of Israel God never at any time loses complete control even over the most perverse actions of his enemies or his people. To impress this truth upon us the psalmist affirms that in the midst of all the sinful tendencies and actions of his people, God holds on to them so tightly that he keeps the initiative and power always in his own hands. It was he himself, not the elders of Israel and not the Philistines, who ordained that the Ark should be sent into captivity and the Temple of Shiloh destroyed.

Not only was God deserted and humiliated when the Ark was taken captive, he was also left by himself alone to work a way through this crisis into the future for his hopeless and dejected people. A later prophet, describing events in his own day, heard God's relevant word: "I looked, but there was no one to help . . . so my own arm brought me victory, and my wrath upheld me" (Isa. 63:5, RSV). In the long run God has to depend on his own zeal and power when others fail, faint, and grow weary. People like Hannah and Samuel are to be admired and praised for their faithful waiting and praying, but when the final issues are to be faced it is only because God's heart still burns when others have grown cold, and God's resources are still boundless when others have spent everything, that his people are brought through in the end.

Glory in and through Shame

The most remarkable feature of the story is that it was precisely *within* and through all these circumstances of deep humiliation that God finally vindicated his name and restored completely the honor of his Ark. He did not exempt either the Ark or himself from any indignity the situation brought upon it. He did not seek to avoid entering any of the shame heaped on him by the faithlessness of his own people and the mocking pride of the Philistines. He did not try to violate the limitations that he had accepted when he made the Ark the sign of himself. It burned with no protective miraculous fire to make people afraid of it. It was never made to appear to be anything more than it ever was, a simple box. In delivering it from the enemy God achieved the extraordinary triumph of his power and wisdom, acting at the same time with great gentleness and in apparently meek submission to the will of those who held it in captivity.

When we read certain passages in the Old Testament they inevitably remind us of Christ. When we read, for example, the description of the suffering servant in the fifty-third chapter of Isaiah, or the account in the twenty-second psalm of a faithful soul undergoing dereliction before God, or the story of Isaac following his father to Mount Moriah and obediently hewing the wood for his sacrifice, our minds inevitably move towards what happened in Jerusalem on Good Friday. It is not surprising that also in this very simple and moving Old Testament story of the Ark in its captivity, our minds should begin to dwell on what happened when Jesus was deserted by his friends, taken captive, mocked, and sent in his humiliation from one place of judgment to another — God's glory in humiliation!

It is a remarkable feature of the story that, just as Jesus' captors were made uneasy when he was delivered into their hands (cf. John 18:6-8), so the Philistines time and again were made uneasy with the Ark in their midst. The plagues that seemed to accompany it on its journey from city to city reinforced the message of the signs that had been given in the temple of Dagon. They were too afraid to try to destroy it. They did not dare to keep it. Their problem was — how to send it back.

The story of the exodus of the Ark is, indeed, to be regarded as no less marvelous than that of the exodus of the children of Israel from bondage in Egypt. The *"priests and the diviners"* of the Philistines were called together to give their advice. God worked as we often find him doing when pagan emperors had to make decisions that affected his people. He put in their minds the thoughts he wanted them to think, and made them take the path that would best serve his own purposes. Of course they imagined that their plans and schemes were their own. They consulted the books and sat in council together. God controlled their tongues and the debates and made sure that the decision served his purposes (cf. Prov. 16:9).

The five kings of the Philistines were inclined to take the advice of their counselors. "The king's heart is a stream of water in the hand of the LORD; he turns it wherever he will" (Prov. 21:1). We are actually told that the chief motive for the priests and diviners of the Philistines was to *"give glory to the God of Israel"* (6:5). They remembered, and pondered over the reports they had heard, the word he had spoken and the things he had done in Egypt. They knew that disaster had followed disaster only because Pharaoh, king of Egypt, had hardened his heart in folly against the God of Israel. In humility they took the warning and hoped that the Lord would be more merciful to them, if they let the Ark go in peace. Wiser and more responsive to the word of God than the elders of Israel had been to Samuel's preaching, they issued what can be interpreted as a call to national repentance. They sent home the Ark of God with honor.

Exodus — with Superstition

Of course it was sent back with superstition as well as with honor. The Philistine magicians believed that the plagues that had visited their cities when the Ark was taken round had been caused by rodents. Its nastiest symptom had been a mass of tumors erupting on the body. They believed that the sending away of five golden mice and five golden tumors would ensure that the plague would depart as the Ark departed. The gift of gold would surely appease the anger of the Lord God of Israel. The new cart would be a further sign of respect, and they would put his power to the final and difficult test. The milch cows were to be separated from their calves and yoked to the cart. It was then to be directed on the road towards Israel. The calves would be taken from their mothers and shut up in a byre. If the cows obeyed their natural instinct, of course no force on earth would be able to drive them to Israel. If the God of Israel were the powerful God that his word proclaimed, then let him show it and let him guide his Ark to where it truly belonged.

There are certain heathen practices and customs with which God never compromises — such as witchcraft and child-sacrifice. Yet it is in keeping with his character and wisdom to accept the service of pagan superstition, and sometimes to humor those who ask or expect from him some sign that accords with the belief in magic. The Bible shows that when he wanted to give guidance, especially to people in heathen countries, he was never too superior and exalted to use the same means of communication as the wise men and magicians could understand. In Egypt he gave important guidance through the dreams given to Pharaoh and interpreted by Joseph as if he had some extraordinary gift of divination. Nebuchadnezzar, king of Babylon, was also spoken to and guided by God not only in dreams (cf. Dan. 2 and 4), but when he consulted his augurers on his military expedition: "the king of Babylon stands at the parting of the way, at the fork in the two roads, to use divination; he shakes the arrows, he consults the teraphim, he inspects the liver. Into his right hand comes the lot for Jerusalem" (Ezek. 21:21-22).

It is when we finally think over this whole incident, asking ourselves what it has to tell us today about God, that we begin to grasp an important aspect of the gospel. God did not allow the Ark to be destroyed because he could not bear to allow Israel to destroy itself. He held on to the Ark in its humiliation because he was holding on to Israel in its shame and apostasy. Moreover, he held on to Israel because he was holding on to his purpose that the world (including you and me!) should be redeemed through the Christ who was to come — his dear son! When we think it over, of course God could not do anything other than hold on to his people. Had he not pledged himself to do so, not only to the founders of the nation, but to trusting people like Hannah and Samuel to whom he had repeated his promises? He had put too much into the life of this one nation, now to let it go. He had to hold on to Israel even for his own sake, said Ezekiel (Ezek. 36:20-23).

Yet his decision to hold on to his people was made at great sacrificial cost to himself. It was the later prophets of Israel who began gradually to understand what it cost him to refrain from vindicating himself other than by continuing to love Israel and humankind, and to bear in himself the shame and agony in remaining forever Israel's God and ours (cf. Hos. 11:8-9).

> How can I give you up, Ephraim?
> How can I hand you over, O Israel?
> How can I make you like Admah?
> How can I treat you like Zeboiim?
> My heart recoils within me;
> my compassion grows warm and tender.
> I will not execute my fierce anger;
> I will not again destroy Ephraim;
> for I am God and no mortal.   (Hos. 11:8-9)

The Two Milch Cows

The two milk cows deserve separate and special mention. They *"went straight in the direction of Bethshemesh along one highway, lowing as they went; they turned neither to the right nor to the left, and the lords of the Philistines went after them as far as the border of Bethshemesh"* (6:12). How important it was that these dumb animals should be willing to stand in and to face the task given to them and do it well! God needed some mediator to take back the Ark. The Philistines were too afraid to risk remaining near it. The men of Israel were unwilling or unable to come and fetch it. It was as if the cattle recognized the emergency and the importance of their task, and knew whom they were serving. It was to them a costly journey. They made it *"lowing as they went,"* for they remembered their calves at home. Yet they denied themselves and in strict obedience to their maker refused ever to veer from the one straight track. They put us to shame when we read of them. We can feel the force of Isaiah's reproach to the disobedient and ungrateful people of his own generation. "The ox knows its owner, and the donkey its master's crib; but Israel does not know, my people do not understand" (Isa. 1:3).

Preachers have sometimes praised the colt on which Jesus sat when he entered Jerusalem on Palm Sunday. It had never been broken in, yet it recognized whom it was serving and it became as meek and obedient as the king who sat on it. It took him on the way he was destined to go. These two cows are surely its forerunners in the same holy service. One feels that among the animals in the new heaven and the new earth there must be an honored place for those two cows who seem in the end to have dumbly stood in the field by the rock and offered themselves to be sacrificed like the ram caught in a thicket on Mount Moriah.

Here we have a reminder of a theme that occasionally appears in the Bible elsewhere — that the redemption which is to be achieved as the promises of Israel's God are fulfilled will involve the whole animal creation as well as the human family: that in the new age to come "the wolf shall live with the lamb, and the leopard shall lie down with the kid, the calf and the lion and the fatling together, and a little child shall lead them" (Isa. 11:6).

The Ark in the Harvest Field

"Now the people of Bethshemesh were reaping their wheat harvest in the valley. When they looked up and saw the ark, they went with rejoicing to meet it" (v. 13).

How picturesque is the scene on this harvest field! It was just on the borderline between Philistine territory and Israel. The people had for more than six months been harassed by enemy raiders. They were defenseless, dependent only on divine protection. They had been asking questions. Was not the destruction of their Temple, the death of their priests, and the capture of the Ark a sign that God had deserted them? They were especially uncertain as they tried to harvest their crop. The enemy could now come and seize what they had ready in the field before they were able to hide what they needed for the coming winter. No doubt they had sentries on the border to alert them, and they were terrified to hear that there was movement towards them from the enemy's territory. They lifted up their eyes to the distant edge of the valley and they saw silhouetted against the sky the figures of the Philistine kings and their banner. Soon, however, they saw that the figures were motionless and were simply watching a cart yoked to cattle on the road, wending its way towards them. Perhaps it was something being sent to act as a decoy and to trap them! It took time to recognize what it might be. Then they saw — the Ark! Their shouts of joy brought others running with them to meet it where the cattle stopped at the great stone in the field of Joshua.

The scene is not only dramatic but also full of meaning. For at least some of them in that harvest field their joy that year had been incomplete, unsatisfying — and they were beginning to understand why. They had no Ark in their midst in the Temple — no sign of God's redeeming presence and power! They were beginning to understand what it had meant in their ordinary daily life, and especially at its highest point in the harvest field. In the return of the Ark they suddenly saw that their God had not forsaken them.

How much we still need today the insight that was theirs with such conviction at that moment — that the God of the creation was also the God of their redemption, and moreover, that the God of their redemption was also the God of their creation! The natural world around us is full of wonderful things. It has variety and beauty and is designed to meet all our needs; it is given to us freely to use and enjoy. But we can only fully enjoy what is given us in nature if we first know something of the redeeming love that has delivered us from the evils that otherwise corrupt, steal, and destroy what is good. How much it can transform and stabilize all our justifiable natural joys and celebrations in life — our harvests and birthdays, our marriages or sports — when we begin to see in our midst the Ark of the redeeming God.

CHAPTER 7

The Days of Samuel

1 Samuel 6:19–7:17

The Narrative

Even among the people of Bethshemesh who gave such a reverent and warm welcome to the Ark, there were now, as always, those who had no respect for its holiness or understanding of what it stood for. They desecrated it and, under the judgment it brought on them, refused to restore it to a central place in their national life and disposed of it where they believed it would do no more harm. It was in the purpose of God that for many years from this time forth, Samuel's wisdom as judge and ruler, and his prophetic word, should control things in Israel; and we are finally told how for a long time Israel prospered under him. We are also told of how God initiated this important, though interim, period in Israel's history by as miraculous a defeat of the Philistines as that experienced under the leadership of Moses at the Red Sea, and of how Samuel set up the stone *"Ebenezer"* as a memorial of it.

Samuel's Task and Achievement

Samuel's influence over affairs in Israel was so powerful during the reign of Saul and the early years of David's life, that we are apt to think of these days as the great period of his life's work. We must not forget, however, that what he did in those early days of the monarchy was done in the evening of his life — after he had grown old (cf. 8:5) and retired. The greatest part of his life-work was completed long before Saul appeared on the public scene. His period of full ascendancy in Israel began only after the shameful defeat of Israel at Aphek, and it lasted for a period of slightly more than twenty years. During that time he accomplished his life-work as a prophet and judge in Israel, completely transforming the whole of its religious and political life. With the help of God he did it alone, for the whole eldership as well as the priesthood had been discredited in the aftermath of Aphek.

To help us appreciate what he achieved we are reminded, at the beginning of our present account, of the reception the men of Bethshemesh gave to the Ark soon after it was returned by the Philistines. They treated it despicably, and when God in judgment came to its defense and gave a clear witness to its continuing holiness in his sight, they reacted merely by getting some of its adherents who had not lost their former zeal for the Lord to take the thing away and put it where they could be left in peace. They were typical of the large majority of the Israel that Samuel had to face. We have to recall also how, for a very long time before Samuel had been raised up to preach it, the word of God had been *"rare"* in Israel (3:1) and the minds of the people had been open mainly to pagan falsehood. Moreover, under Philistine bondage they had been robbed of their former wealth and were thus deprived of all worthy cultural development. They were tempted to bitterness and despair.

For many years, therefore, Samuel was forced simply to work only by faith, seeing no immediate results, having to wait with patience. It was only after several hard years of tactful leadership, pastoral care, and constant prayer (7:5) that he was able to reap what he had sown. The harvest was rich and its fruit endured. We are given enough important detail to form a clear picture of how Samuel took his stand, set about this work, and achieved his triumph. The writer, of course, intends that at this point in the narrative we should not forget the prayers of Hannah which are now answered, and her hopes which are now fulfilled.

"A Movement throughout Israel"

Samuel must from the beginning of his ascendancy have known that there was a twofold task before him. As God's prophet he undoubtedly longed for the time and opportunity to preach effectively so that Israel could be brought, in a movement of repentance and renewal, back to the truth and service of God. Moreover, as Israel's judge and leader he had been raised up also to lead his people out of bondage to their oppressors and set them free among the nations to fulfill their God-given destiny. He had to wait long before he received a sign from God that the time was ripe for him to take any such decisive action: "a long time passed, some twenty years," during which he was called to concentrate on winning the shattered confidence of the people, by moving quietly from place to place in their midst, hearing and judging in local disputes, and teaching about their nation's history. To keep himself going he accepted small payments for services he rendered, and kindled the devotion of those who came around by offering sacrifice at hallowed local shrines (cf. the description in chapter 9).

The sign that the time was ripe for him to begin to take more decisive action was when he began to notice a decided change in the social climate and the attitude of individuals here and there to his appeals and his teaching. *"All the house of Israel lamented after the Lord,"* we are told (7:2).

The New English Bible gives a very apt translation of this expression in verse 2 when it tells us that *"there was a movement throughout Israel to follow the Lord."* At first the *"movement"* would be fugitive. The influence of an older generation began to wane. New attitudes would begin to shape the response of a rising generation to their tragic situation and to the problems of life. The thought would arise and develop that it was because they had departed from God and despised his ways and laws that disaster had come. The Jerusalem Bible in its translation of this passage says that the people *"longed for Yahweh."*

We are meant to notice how widespread it was. *"All the house of Israel lamented"* (v. 2). It was not confined to elite or militant groups here and there who met together especially to build themselves up and encourage each other over against a hard wall of indifference on the part of the massive majority. We have a parallel to what happened in Nehemiah, chapter 8. After a long period of indifference, Ezra found the situation around him so changed that when he set up his pulpit to preach before the people at the Water Gate, all Israel "gathered together into the square before the Water Gate" (8:1), and the "ears of all the people were attentive" (8:3). No doubt, of course, in Samuel's time the people met in groups to discuss their affairs, ideas, and feelings (cf. Mal. 3:16). These were not, however, gatherings apart from, but within what was happening *"throughout Israel."*

Samuel, of course, at first, would recognize its possible superficiality. A sense of sorrow even about our sins or spiritual state, however deeply felt, is not repentance. Samuel knew that even while they were possessed by this sorrow the people, often individually and in secret, still involved themselves in the orgies of Baal worship. Certainly those former exciting practices were losing their meaning and attraction and often evoked merely a sense of shame. Even as they worshiped at the forbidden shrines they were longing for better things, and beginning to have thoughts of how much more stable and satisfying life would have been had they not forsaken the Lord (cf. Jer. 3:23). But they were still merely movements of desire and thought with no control over will or action.

Yet he recognized finally the situation before him might be the beginning of the great work of God for which he had been praying and waiting. He judged it to be the sign that Israel was by God's grace ready to respond, to listen seriously as never before to the word of God, to a call for a true repentance, and to give to God what it would cost.

Repentance!

Then it happened! Wherever he preached Samuel's word went home with such convincing power to the minds and hearts of those who heard him that there was no delay. Israel repented, and a remarkable and unique renewal in their religious and moral life took place.

The preaching of the word of God suddenly seemed to come into its own. *"Samuel said to all the house of Israel, '... put away the foreign gods and the Astartes from among you. Direct your heart to the LORD, and serve him only. ....' So Israel put away the Baals and the Astartes, and they served the LORD only"* (vv. 3-4). We cannot help thinking of the news from Psalm 33:9: "He spoke, and it came to be; he commanded, and it stood firm." The psalmist was extolling the power of the word of God in bringing light out of darkness and order out of chaos. The Lord said, "Let there be ... and there was ..." (Gen. 1:3, 6, 9, etc.). Our writer seems to be deliberately making the claim that God endowed the preached word of Samuel with the same creative power as he himself used and manifested in the creation of the universe. God was himself present with redeeming and creative power when the word was preached.

Certain features of the repentance Samuel called for are worth our notice. He was not content merely to denounce the sin of idolatry and to call for purity of worship within the heart. He called not simply for one great act of self-renunciation but for the acceptance of a whole new way of life under God's control. He expected a passionate and drastic change, especially at the point at which they had done most wrong to God's love. His call was for drastic action against the multitude of man-made idols that abounded in their local shrines and in their homes. These were to be *"put away"* or *"banished"* (NEB). Did Samuel not tell them the story of how Dagon had been smashed to pieces when the Ark of the Lord entered Dagon's temple? "Repentance unto life," says the Westminster Shorter Catechism, "is a saving grace, whereby a sinner, out of a true sense of his sin, and apprehension of the mercy of God in Christ, doth, with grief and hatred of his sin, turn from it unto God, with full purpose of, and endeavor after, new obedience."

It is our belief that there was little difference, in the rich and powerful inward reality of what happened then, from what often happens today in response to evangelical preaching. That Israel *"served the LORD only"* meant not only for each individual the dethronement of all pagan gods; it meant that the self which then, as now, tends to make our wholehearted service of one God impossible, must be totally dethroned in one decisive inner act of self-renunciation. Men and women "surrendered" or "yielded" themselves to God. The invitation to *"direct your heart to the LORD"* was a call to make this surrender continuously in the cultivation of devotional habit. The Jerusalem Bible translates this phrase as *"set your heart on Yahweh."* Different aspects of what this devotional practice involved in Old Testament times are brought before us here and there. One of the psalmists describes it as "holding in mind" his "great acts" (78:7, NEB). Another confesses, "On the glorious splendor of your majesty, and on your wondrous works, I will meditate" (143:5).

It was of course God's redeeming love for his people in

the miraculous work of redemption that was always the central focus of their mind, but time and again, recognizing that all the glory of nature was work inspired by the same love, the psalmists gloried in the whole wonder of creation (cf. Ps. 19). They found moreover that they could set the Lord before them by meditating on his law (cf. Ps. 119), which they believed imaged his own inner nature. They found what gave their lives true direction and peace in this practice. To these men the quality of our life and our stability in the service of God depends on what we "set before our eyes" (cf. Ps. 101:3). "I have set the LORD always before me: because he is at my right hand, I shall not be moved" (Ps. 16:8, AV). The ninety-first psalm is a series of rich and unforgettable promises from God which, we are assured, will be fulfilled in the day-to-day life of anyone who by *setting* his love on God (v. 14, AV) thus *abides* under the shadow of the Almighty.

We have to remember that they made such efforts towards God only because they already knew he was there seeking them. He was seeking them because he had forgiven them and was calling them back to himself. Moreover, it was his forgiving presence that was both inspiring and creating the repentance they were being enabled by grace to offer. In the Bible the possibility of repentance is always linked inseparably with the possibility of forgiveness. It is only because we are forgiven that we can repent. It is only because we repent that we are forgiven.

Mizpah

Mizpah was a place where the tribes of Israel had at times met to make common decisions of national importance. When he summoned all Israel to gather there Samuel no doubt had in mind the kind of great national gathering of men, women, and children that Moses had summoned, not only at Mount Horeb, but also in the land of Moab when the whole nation presented itself "before the LORD" (cf. Deut. 29:10-11). These people from their scattered homes and villages had in the days of Samuel for years been deprived of their Temple as a religious center, and had thus lacked the strength that came to them from realizing their membership in this national religious community with its great traditions and greater destiny. Here was a gathering that would help them express their new-found unity with each other in the Lord and experience what it meant to worship in the midst of a great congregation. It set the seal to everything Samuel had worked and prayed for in his preaching.

On this great occasion God seems to have inspired the people to give the same kind of honor to Samuel (cf. Exod. 14:30-31; Josh. 4:14) as they had given to Moses and Joshua in their great days, and he crowned his leadership with the same remarkable success.

The celebration from the beginning reflected the repentance that had so characterized their response to his work. That they *"drew water and poured it out before the LORD"* (7:6) was a sign of the pouring out of the heart to God in penitence (cf. Lam. 2:19) and of their willingness to devote themselves without reserve to God's service. Their fasting was an outward sign of their willingness to deny their own wills and desires in the service of the Lord.

In summoning Israel to Mizpah, however, Samuel had more in mind than religious celebration. He believed that this people, having begun to realize their true human dignity and their calling to serve God and him alone, would want now to become free from every kind of bondage, political or social, that might hinder them both in the way of life to which the Lord had called them, and in the fulfillment of the destiny promised to their father Abraham. Of course there was risk in calling men and women and children together en masse with no army and few weapons. The Philistines would be provoked. Samuel was certain that God was leading him, and would honor his obedience. He anticipated the attack. He also anticipated the miraculous deliverance. The assurance he felt was expressed in the very summons to the gathering: *"Gather all Israel at Mizpah, and I will pray to the LORD for you"* (7:5). God had led and delivered defenseless Israel when they had been at the mercy of Pharaoh at the Red Sea, and when they had been in real danger of annihilation by Amalek, simply because Moses had taken his stand and prayed (Exod. 17:9-13).

The political and military implications of the gathering were of course recognized immediately by the Philistines. It was taken by them to be a declaration that their hitherto subdued and submissive enemies were beginning to seek freedom. Israel had again to be crushed and that man Samuel had to be dealt with!

When he saw them beginning to attack, Samuel sacrificed a young lamb, perhaps to remind the people in what direction to orient their hearts, perhaps as an aspect of his appeal to the Lord. Most of the battles Israel engaged in were either won or lost by whatever side first broke into panic. In their previous war with the Philistines they had panicked and lost even before they had begun the battle. In pleading with Samuel to pray for them, Israel knew that if they gave God time and remained courageous all would be well. The miracle happened. *"The LORD thundered loud and long over the Philistines and threw them into confusion. They fled in panic before the Israelites"* (v. 10, NEB). The thunder was timed for exactly the moment when Israel's troops showed up to face the enemy and the battle was ready to open. It was located exactly over the Philistine army and it was of abnormal intensity and duration — loud and long! The Philistines were reminded again of the stories they had heard often of the power of the mighty God who had smitten the Egyptians with every sort of plague (cf. 4:8; 6:6). They gave way in terror and fled. It became a proverb in Israel that as long as there were men like Moses or Samuel standing before God (and perhaps because they were still there before God) Israel's future would be secure (Jer. 15:1).

Ebenezer

"Then Samuel took a stone and set it up between Mizpah and Jeshanah, and called its name Ebenezer; for he said, 'Hitherto the LORD has helped us'" (v. 12, RSV).

The story of what God had done for Israel in rescuing

them from the Philistines must now be given an outstanding place in their memory, and must never be forgotten by succeeding generations. If it had not been for his goodness and mercy *then,* they would not have survived. It was as if God had renewed his promises to them as a people. They could now live to serve him with hope and fresh purpose. In the quiet and ordinary days of their journey ahead he would always be with them, the same in his power and goodness, ready to be tested and trusted.

The name *"Ebenezer"* meant "a stone of help." But it was also the name of the place at which they had gathered when they went out to disgrace themselves and their God before the Philistines at Aphek (cf. 4:1). Samuel indeed chose to set up the stone not at Mizpah but at a place near this fateful field at Ebenezer. The same God who had proved himself faithful to them when he led them in triumph had been no less present with them, faithful and helpful to them, when he let them be defeated! This was Samuel's way of saying to his people: "all things work together for good to them that love God" (Rom. 8:28, AV). We must recognize God's providence and his presence for what has brought us disaster and sorrow as well as for what has brought us liberty and joy.

Samuel's memorial stone was meant to direct the faith and thoughts of his people to a past history much longer and greater than their own experience. By *"Hitherto"* he meant: "from the days of Abraham." By *"us"* he meant: "the people of God from the days of Abraham." What had happened to this one generation at Mizpah was only the most recent in a great series of acts and signs, none of them any less wonderful than the other. Though what they had been through at Mizpah was wonderful indeed, they must learn to rest and nourish their faith on the word that God had spoken to their forefathers over the centuries and on the great deeds by which he had confirmed that word. Their present experience was simply as a fresh echo of the experience of their fathers in the faith. How wise of Samuel! Even though we have continually to verify what we believe by our personal and present experience, how important and steadying it is for us to be able to root our faith in something greater and more certain than simply what has happened within our own personal history, our own souls, and our own environment. Is the whole Bible story not given to us so that we can find example, inspiration, and encouragement in what happened *"hitherto,"* time and again, to our forerunners in the faith?

Certainly this is what the New Testament gospel message seeks continually to do for us. Christ can bring about great changes within our hearts and minds when he enters our lives. We experience within us light instead of darkness, joy instead of despair, freedom instead of fear or bondage. We know inwardly that we have passed from death to life! Yet, as the Gospels are read and preached to us and we receive the sacraments of Christ's grace, do we not find our eyes continually redirected from ourselves towards Christ, to what happened in him and through him? Are we not continually being invited to live by what God did for us once and for all in Christ — in his life, death, and resurrection, rather than by what he has more recently done for us within our own lives and hearts? If we ourselves have experienced an inner rebirth, we owe it to the fact that he was born for us when he brought new life for all humankind into this world at Bethlehem. If we ourselves are freed from our sins to live now for God, it is because he himself once-for-all died and rose again. *"Hitherto"* can become for us an even more important reminder than it was for the Israelites of Samuel's time.

A Final Tribute to Samuel

We must not fail, in closing, to appreciate the faith, wisdom, and insight that the writer attributes to Samuel during the years he was free to govern as he chose.

His stress was on the establishment of justice. He *"judged Israel all the days of his life,"* we are told; *"he judged Israel in all these places."* And again, *"he administered justice"* (vv. 15-17).

The repetition reminds us of one of the great Old Testament pictures of the reign of the promised Messiah: "He will bring forth justice . . . he will faithfully bring forth justice. He will not grow faint or be crushed until he has established justice in the earth" (Isa. 42:1-4). Moreover, it was justice administered within a pastoral context. It was justice to which each individual had free and quick access. The movement around the circuit from Ramah to *"Bethel, Gilgal, and Mizpah . . . [and] back to Ramah"* (vv. 16f.) suggests that each case was heard near its own locality, where the situation was as fully and fairly understood as possible. Even as he administered justice, Samuel proved himself a shepherd to his people — a shepherd who knew and cared about the individual. Samuel's humility is stressed. He had his home at Ramah. It was a *"home,"* one amidst others, not a palace set apart. Samuel was on the same level as all — close to the people. Everyone knew who was coming and going. It was open government. There were no secret hidden deals with a privileged few. No elaborate machinery of government was allowed to develop. None of the trappings found in other countries separated the rulers and judges from the people. Samuel the judge could be easily found, and when they found him they did not find him in state but like a father and ready counselor.

His mother Hannah had felt so deeply in her early home life the injustice of the provocation (1:6) heaped on her because of her childlessness, and her prophetic prayer for Israel dwells on how God *"brings low"* the oppressor and *"raises up the poor from the dust."* It finds its climax in *"the LORD will judge the ends of the earth"* (2:7, 8, 10).

The reader who is familiar with the description in the succeeding chapters of how the kingdom of Israel developed after the days of Samuel will be struck by the contrast between the simple and happy community life described here as flourishing under Samuel and the later state of affairs that prevailed either under David at the height of his power or under his son Solomon. The whole structure of society changed as the monarchy developed. The shepherd-judge living alongside his people and on their level was replaced by a king in a palace, distant from the common people and surrounded by officials and deputies. Everything was on a grander scale; the individual, it seems, shrank in importance. Even the religious life of the community became elaborate. The Ark was restored to the center of the nation's life.

A tabernacle was made for it and a great Temple was planned. A large body of priest-attendants and singers were there to lead the people in what was believed to be a worthy response to God.

Certainly much in this development was given God's blessing. The development of the monarchy, at first resisted by God, was finally accepted and, under David, was even blessed. It may be that God took pleasure in the whole complex development of Israel's religious life. He manifested himself and had fellowship with his people in the midst of it and blessed them through it. In all this he sanctified and blessed Israel's human folly in its preference of the elaborate over the simple, but he did not thereby make what was elaborate of any more real worth than what it replaced.

We must try to understand Samuel in the setting of his day, and we can especially appreciate him as our minds move forward to Christ. He allowed the Ark to remain at Kiriath-jearim and did not try to rebuild a tabernacle for it. Possibly he did not want to take the risk in his day of any return to the pagan ideas that had brought the religious life of the previous generation at Shiloh to such a disastrous end. His people had heard from him, time and again, the living word of God. Therefore they knew that God was near them. They had experienced his hand with mighty power delivering them from evil in answer to prayer. Their faith was nourished in the law and tradition of Moses and the fathers. Samuel visited and set up local altars at which sacrifice would be offered to the Lord — how could they ever forget the sacrifice that had been made at Mizpah and the pleasure God had then taken in what was offered through it?

Thus we need not reproach Samuel in his day for his concern to maintain religious simplicity. We can remember Calvin's dictum that ceremony was the characteristic of Old Testament religion, while simplicity was that of the New. We may be meant to realize that if the Old Testament finds its fulfillment in the New, the New Testament also often shines out in the Old.